AF473779

The miserable Lives of Fabulous Artists

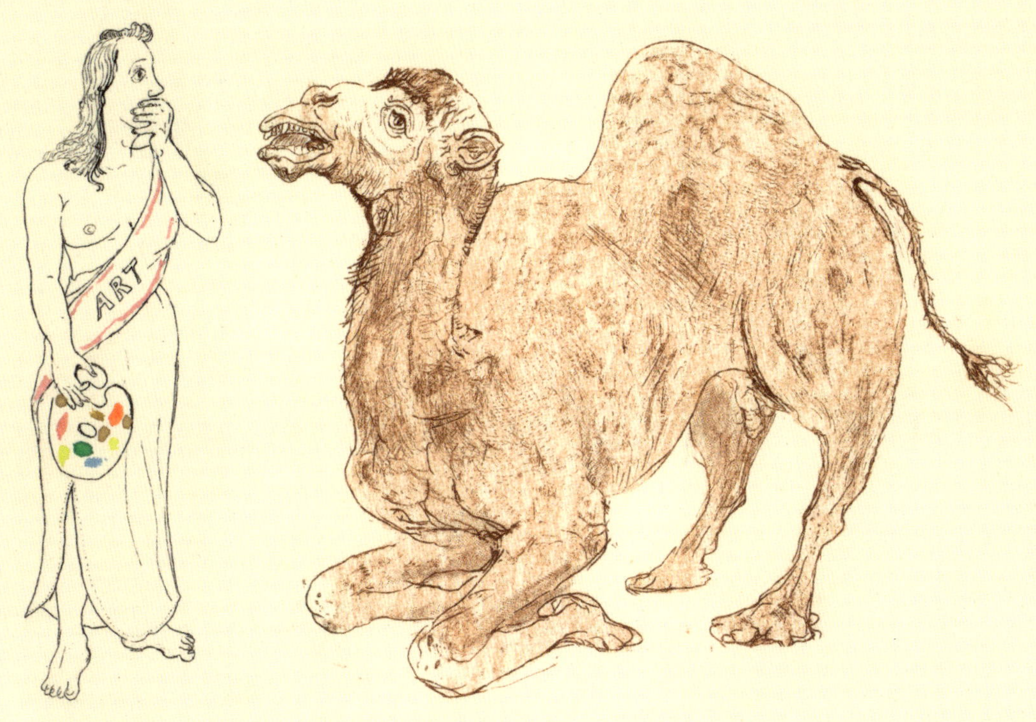

Chris Orr

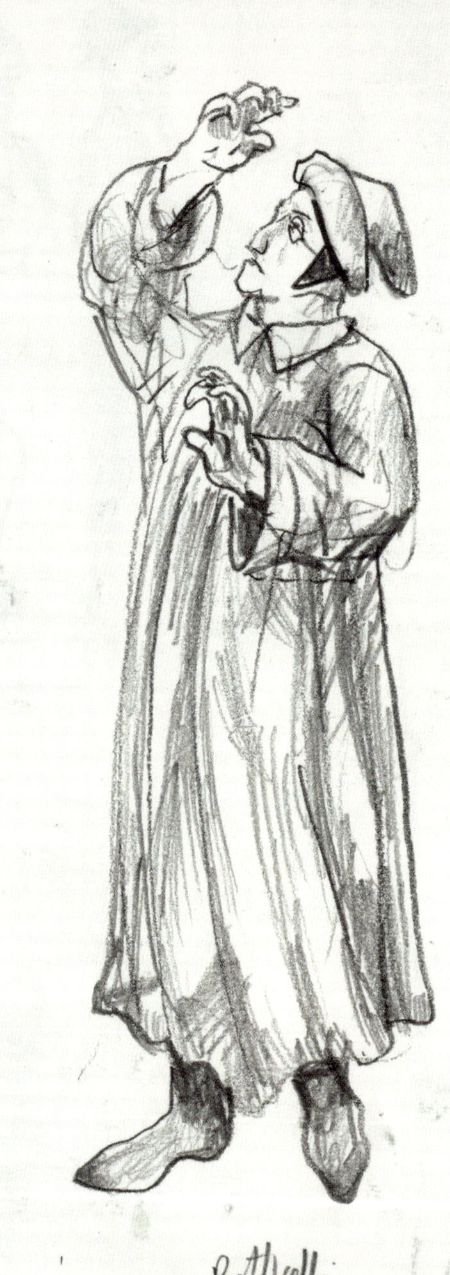

Botticelli

THE LIVES OF THE MOST EXCELLENT PAINTERS

Giorgio Vasari's *Lives of the Most Excellent Painters, Sculptors and Architects*, first published in 1550, is considered the ideological foundation of art historical writing. All artists consider other practitioners as necessary background study, and my *Miserable Lives* is a faint echo of the great tide of art history that washes over us.

My own preoccupation with slightly fictional biographies of artists began with an etching I made in my student days of Gauguin pedalling his paintings around Paris in the snow in a little cart after returning from Tahiti. Subsequently Blake, Ruskin and Dürer have all taken a good thrashing from me. In the *Miserable Lives* I have selected a series of artists to maul, who for one reason or another have had an influence on what I do and what I think. Along with Vasari, Thomas Rowlandson's ironic 'Miseries of London' helped with the title.

Things do not always turn out how you expect and this project is no exception. I write like a painter with a blank canvas in front of me, and I paint like a writer with a great concern for detail. All of my artists are dead, to avoid embarrassment or litigation, and some may have only scraped in to satisfy my obtuse sense of humour. Beryl Cook, for instance, was a Johnny-come-lately purely as a foil to L. S. Lowry.

I can claim to have gone through a very formative time as an artist in the mid-sixties when the world was being turned upside-down. We valued rock and roll above opera, and journalism above literature. We scattered what we inherited, and then picked up the pieces to construct something remarkably like what we had just tried to destroy.

As with all my work, I invite the viewer to 'read' my pictures. So first and foremost this is a picture book, but one where you must study and follow the detail. Flicking through is not allowed. The line between describing in words and images is fluid, but in the later part of the book I expand on some of the thoughts that stimulated the ideas, and in some cases provide a few harder facts.

The project has led me into strange new areas. Trying to see any equation between Constable and Jackson Pollock leads one down – or up – the garden path. Do I really think that artists lead miserable lives? Unlike most other jobs there is no completely private life, because the subject-matter is usually yourself. There are as many different types of artist as there are people, but what they have in common is that they trade in revelation. The picture on the wall is a testament as well as an icon. The study of artists' lives is a major industry, justified by our desire to understand what is behind the work.

Vincent's battle with colour

Vincent Willem van Gogh, painter 1853-1890

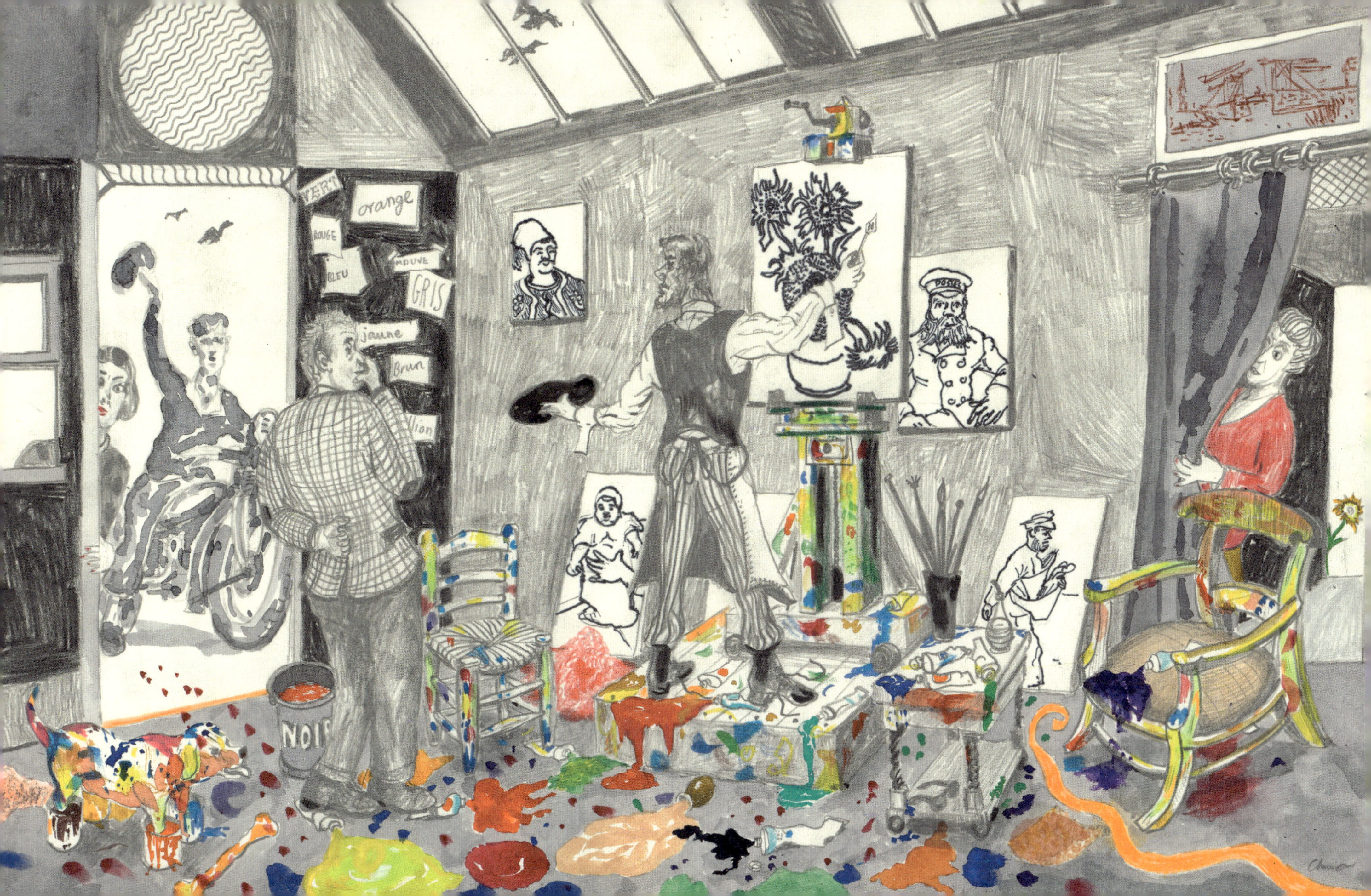

VERT
orange
ROUGE
BLEU
MAUVE
GRIS
jaune
Brun
lion
NOIR

The bits Constable left out

John Constable RA, painter 1776-1837

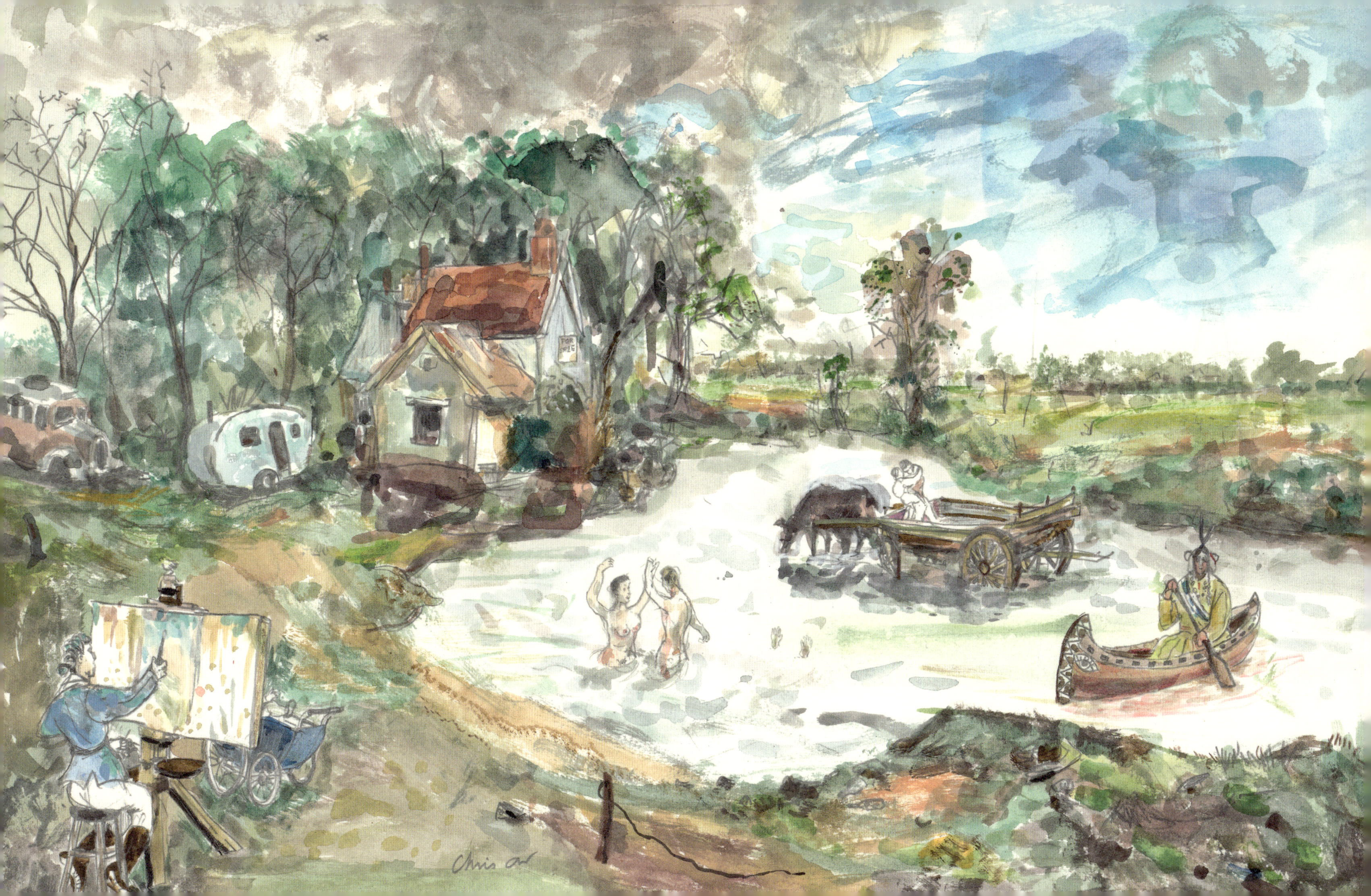
Chris Orr

3

Frida Kahlo
(Diego's dinner)

Frida Kahlo, Magdalena Carmen Frida Kahlo y Calderón
painter 1907 - 1954

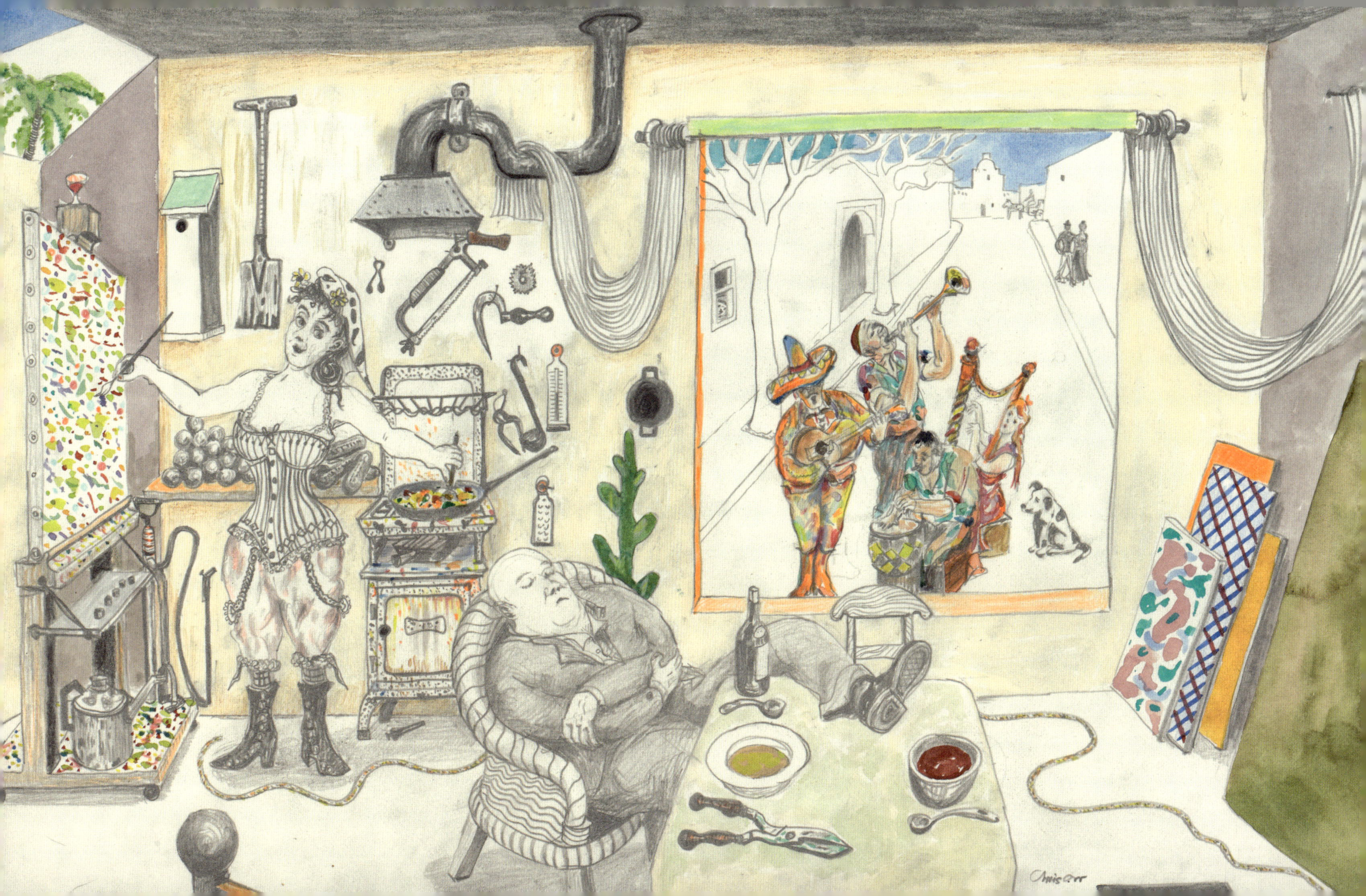

Diego Rivera
(A fry-up for Frida)

Diego María de la Concepción Juan Nepomuceno Estanislao de la Rivera y Barrientos Acosta y Rodríguez

painter 1886–1957

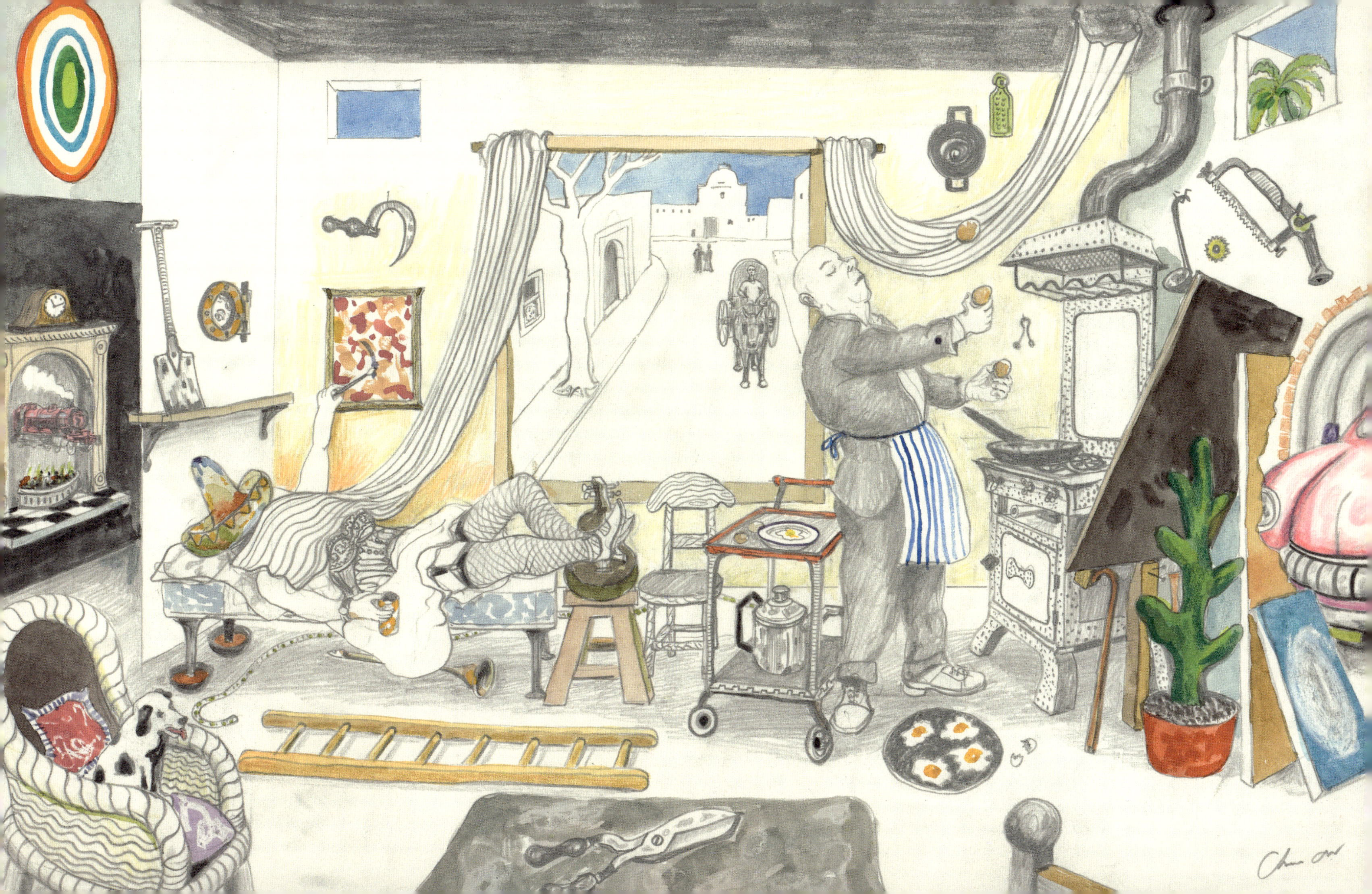

Searching for a lost button at Jackson's

Paul Jackson Pollock, painter 1912-1956

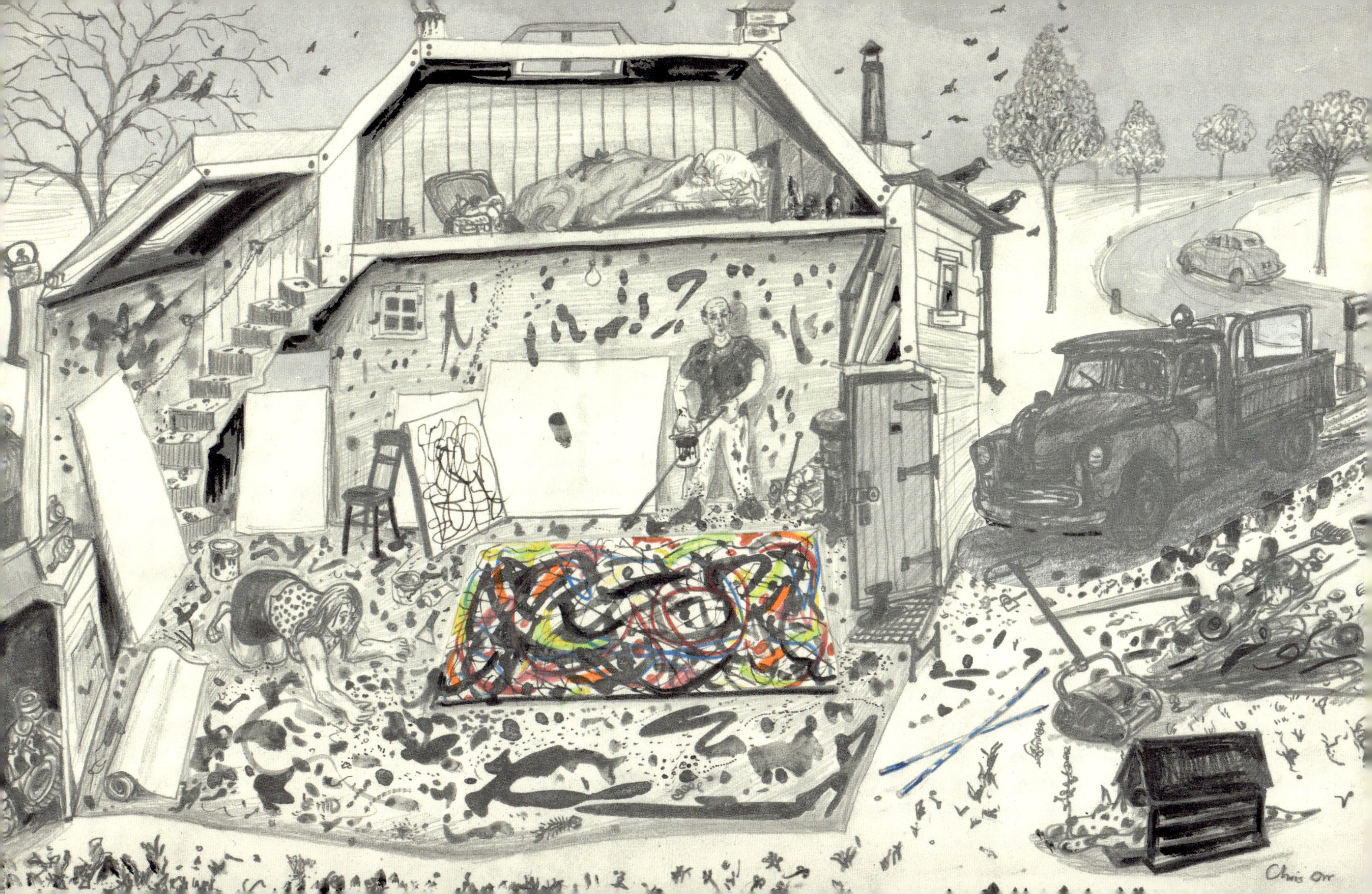
Chris Orr

Angelica Kauffman
is barred from the Royal Academy
life Room

Maria Anna Angelika Kauffmann RA, painter 1741-1807

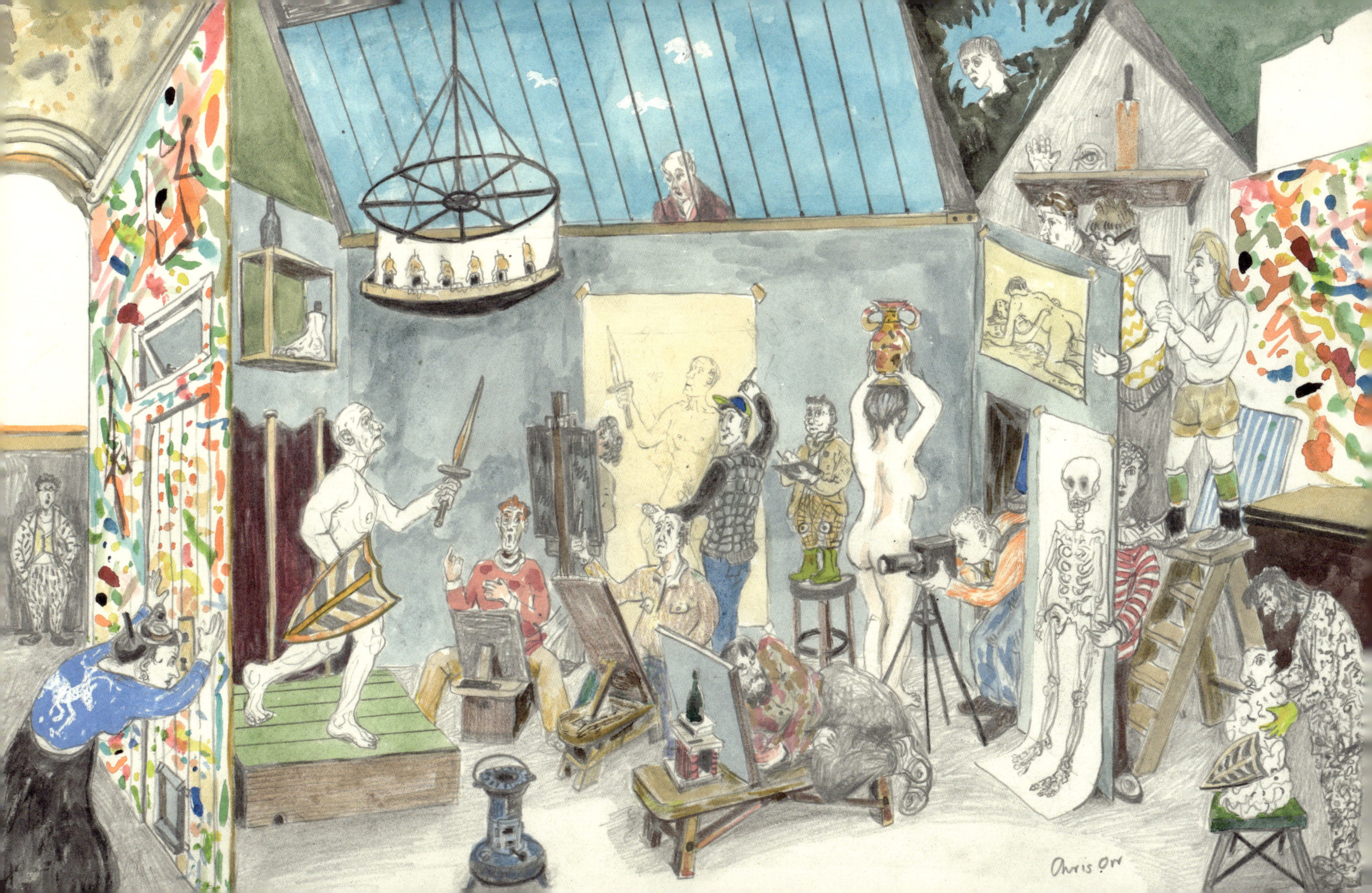
Chris Orr

Picasso's busy day

1881 - 1973

Pablo Ruiz y Picasso, painter, ceramacist, sculptor, printmaker

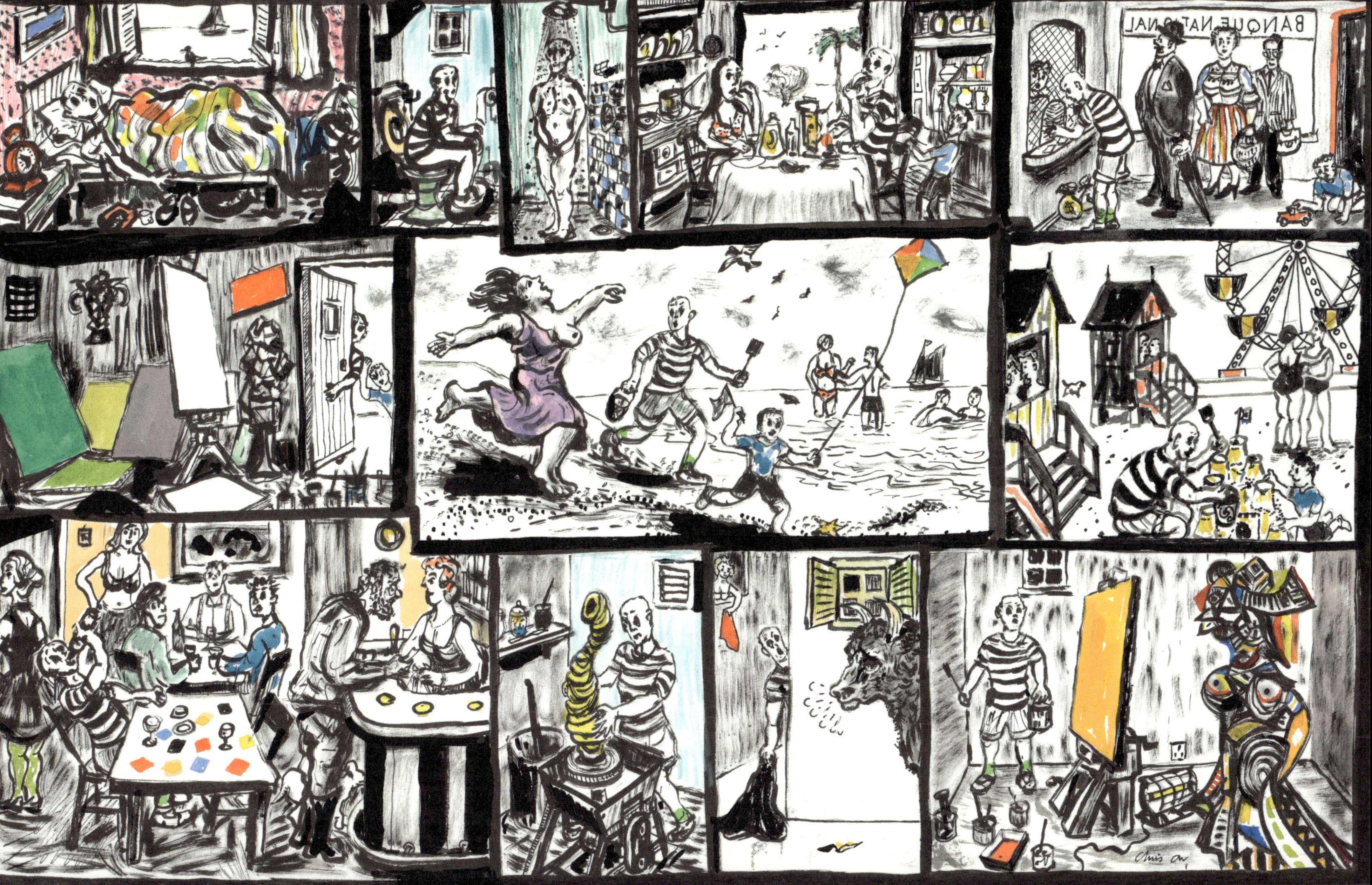
BANQUE NAT NAL

Atkinson Grimshaw
at work in typical conditions

John Atkinson Grimshaw, painter 1836-1893

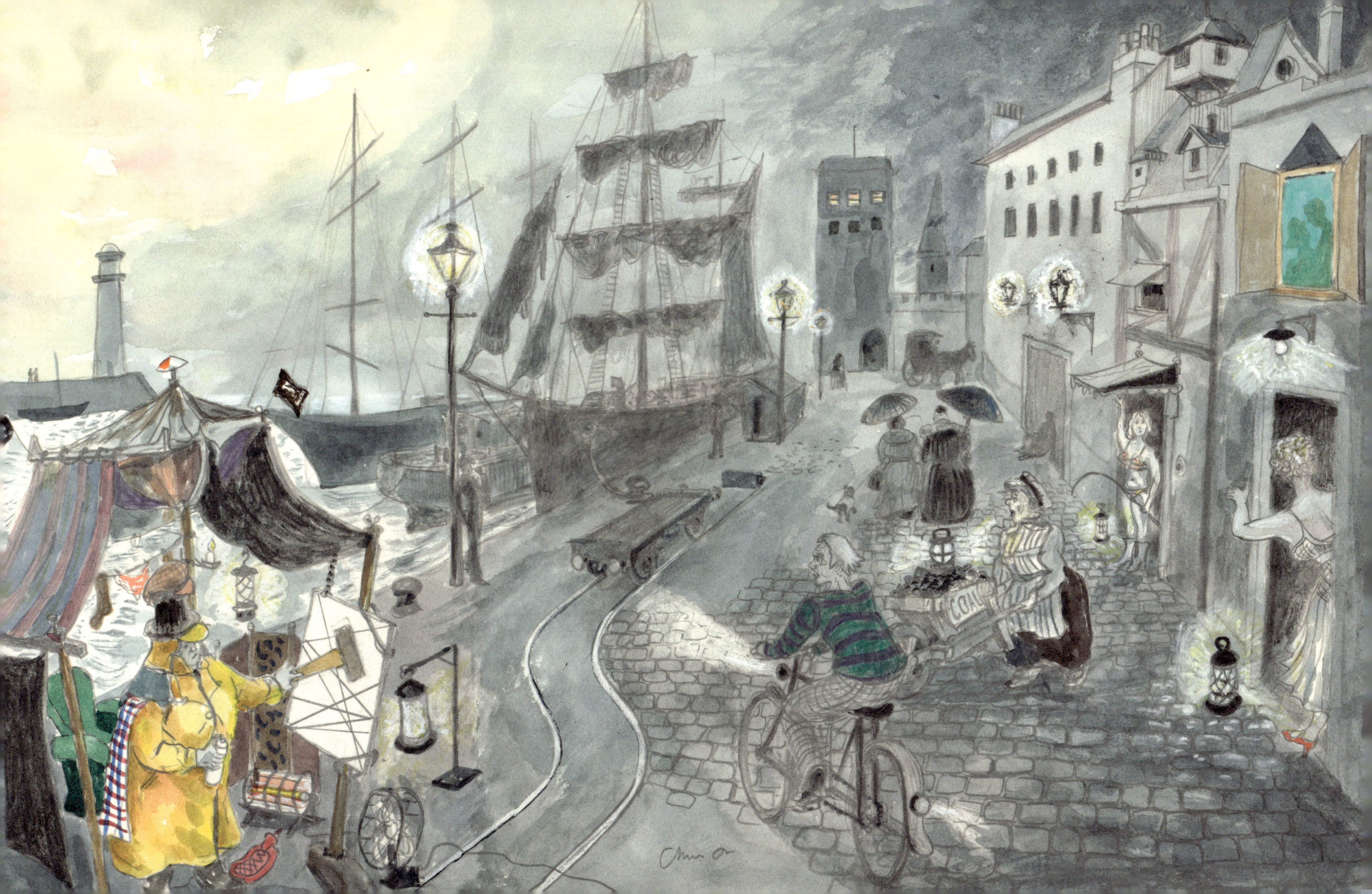
COAL

Dame Laura Knight
Shoplifting in Harrods

Dame Laura Knight RA, painter 1877-1970

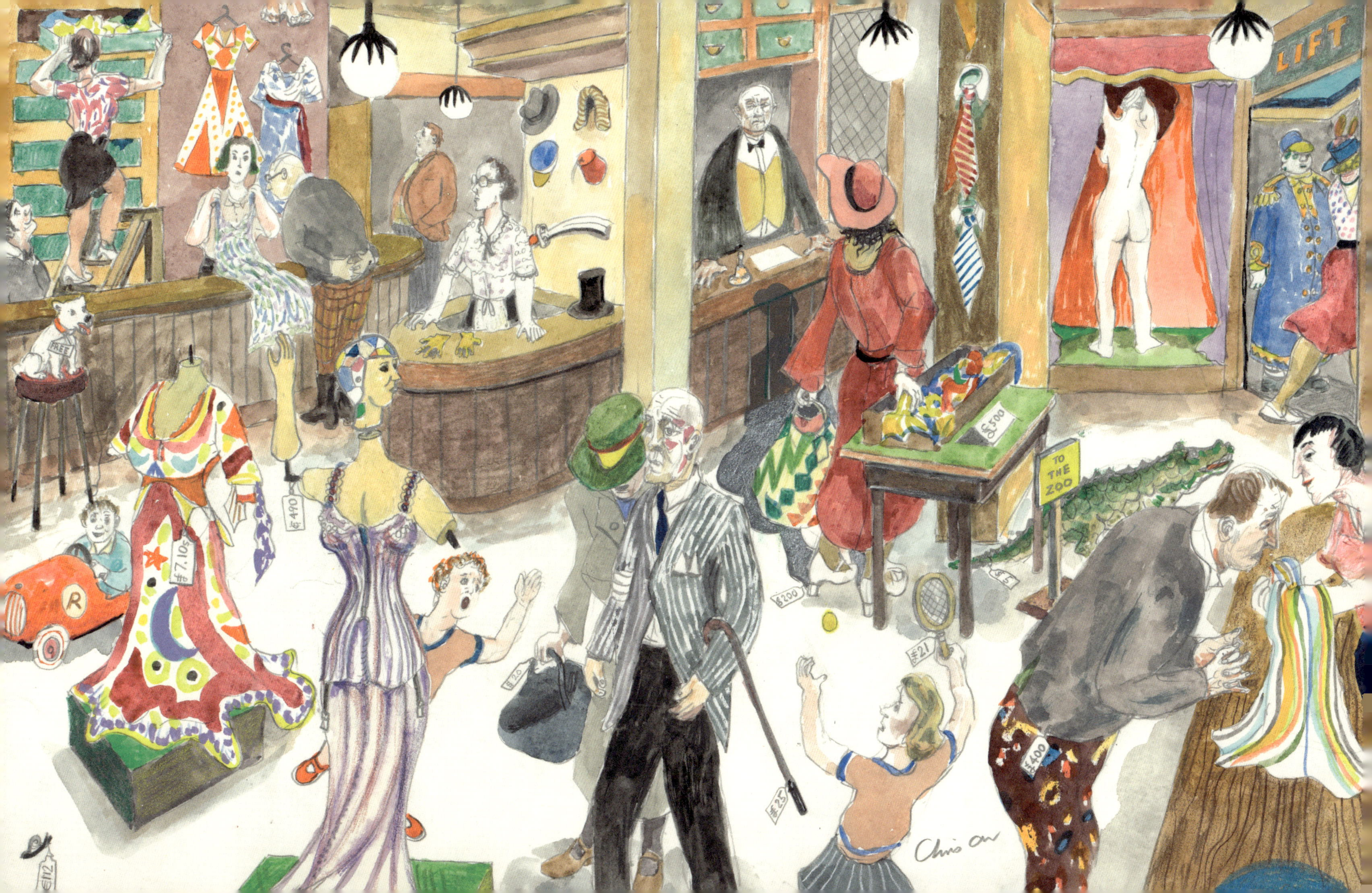

LIFT
TO THE ZOO
FREE
£500
£7.10s
£490
£200
£21
£400
Chris Orr

Munch on holiday

Edvard Munch, painter 1863-1944

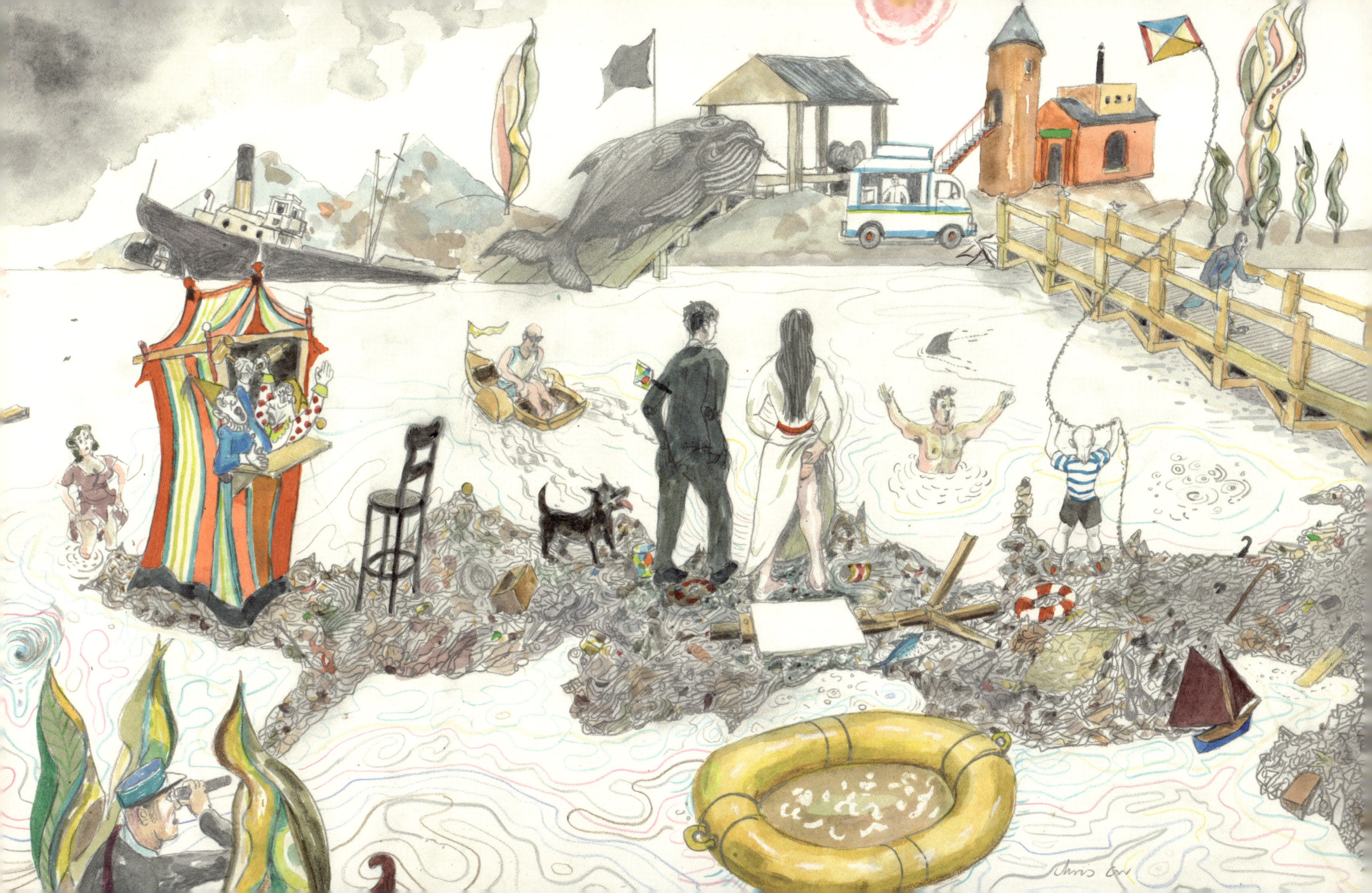

Mr & Mrs Hopper at work

Edward Hopper, painter 1882-1967. Josephine Nivison, painter 1883-1968

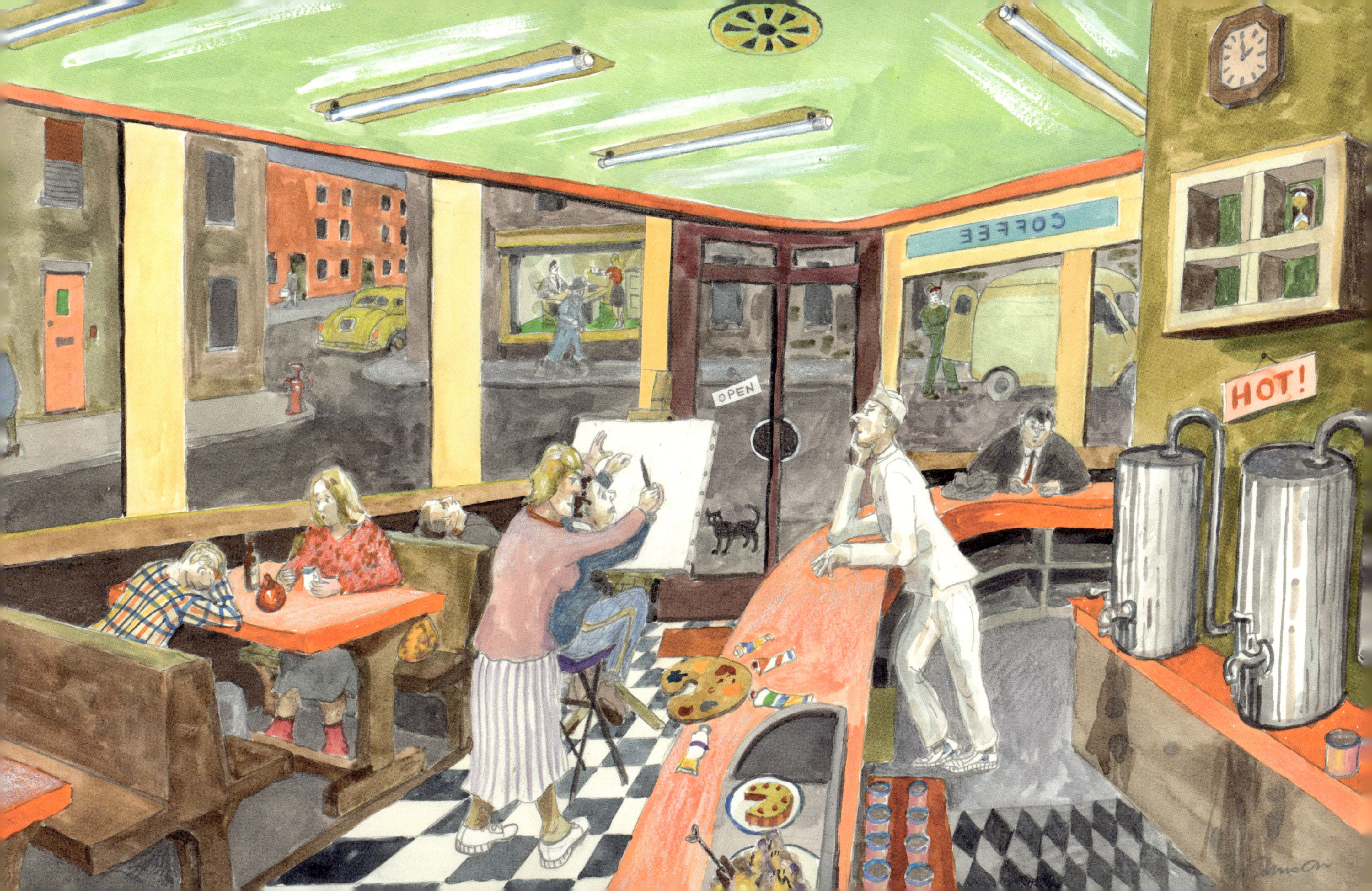
COFFEE
OPEN
HOT!

Foot in the mouth
– James Gillray

James Gillray, engraver 1756–1815

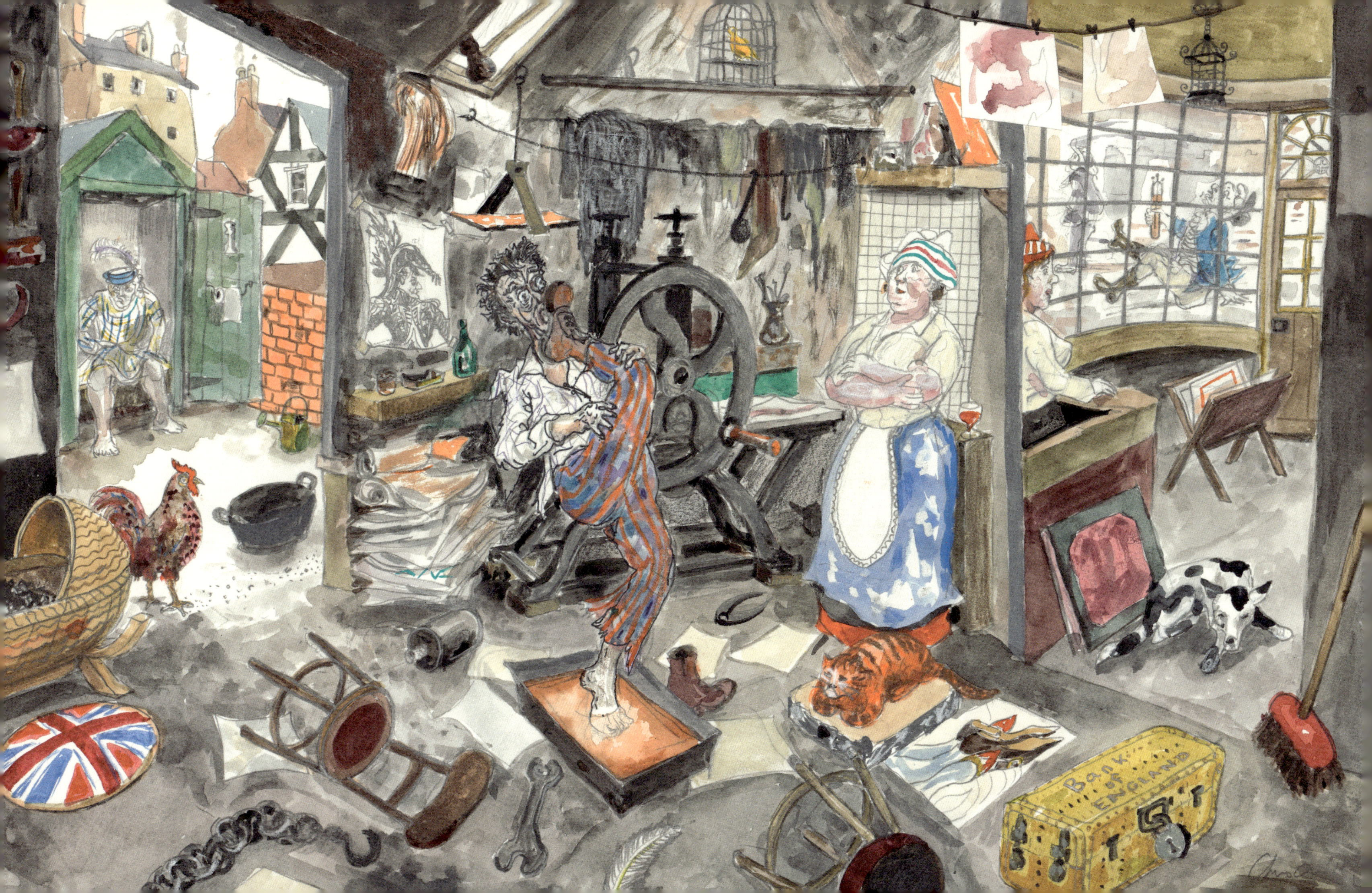
Bank of
ENGLAND

Don't worry Ladies and Gentlemen,
Joseph Beuys has the coyotes
perfectly under control.

Joseph Beuys, sculptor 1921–1986

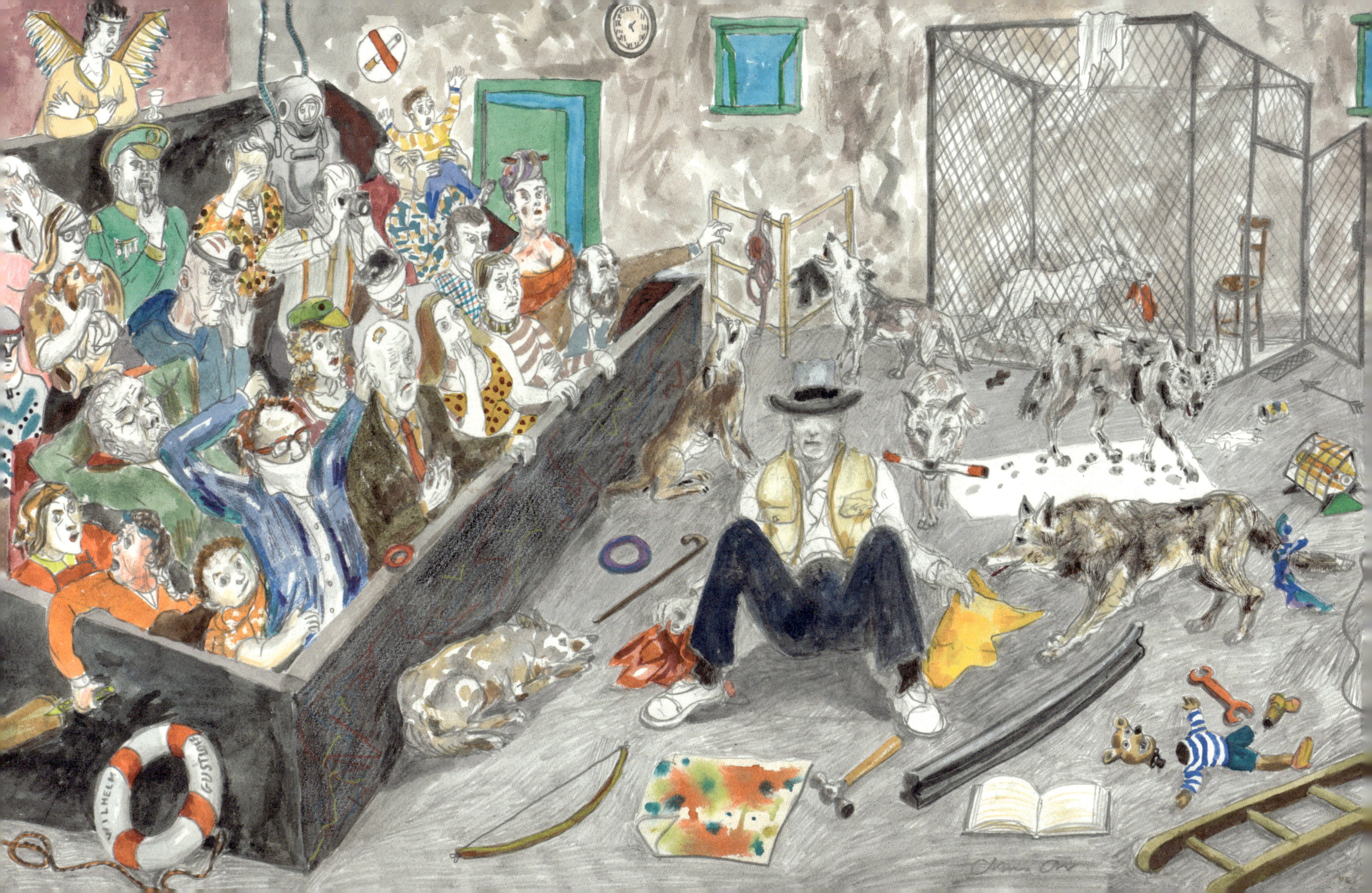
WILHELM
GUSTLOFF

An unfortunate incident in Barbara Hepworth's studio

Jocelyn Barbara Hepworth, sculptor 1903-1975

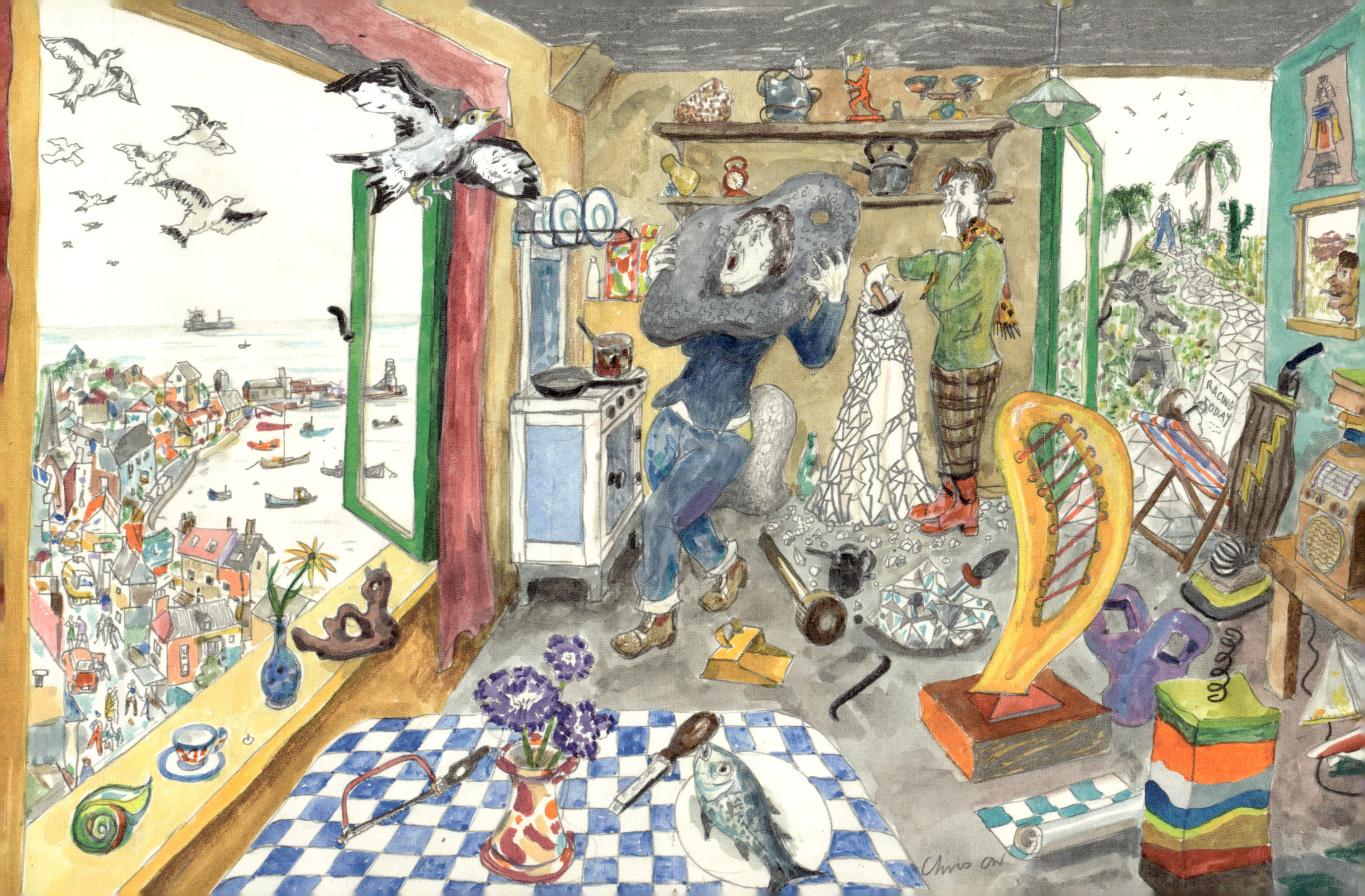
RACING TODAY
Chris Orr

Posada on fire

José Guadalupe Posada, printmaker 1852-1913

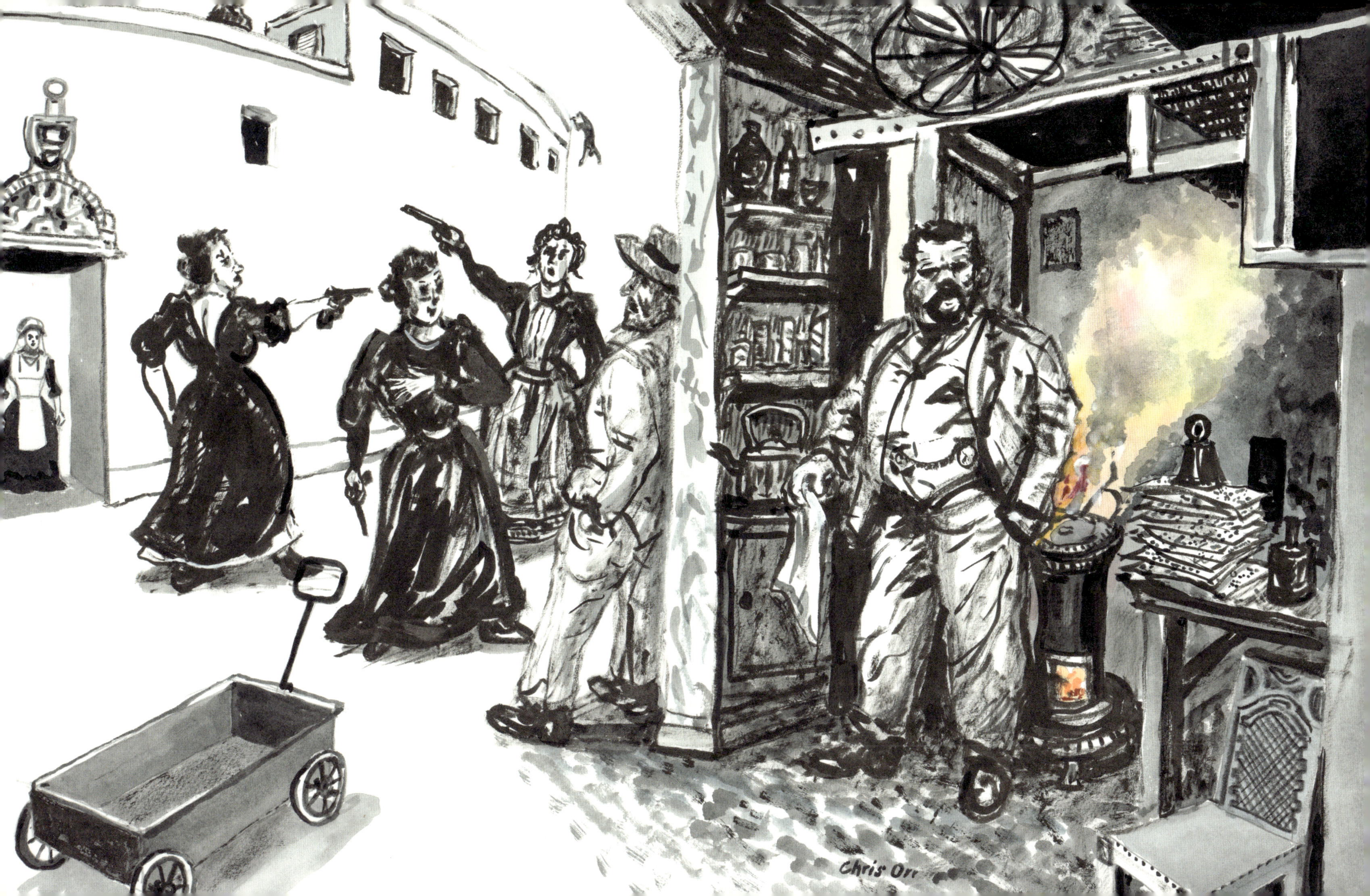
Chris Orr

Walter Sickert finds a fly in his soup

Walter Richard Sickert RA, painter 1860-1942

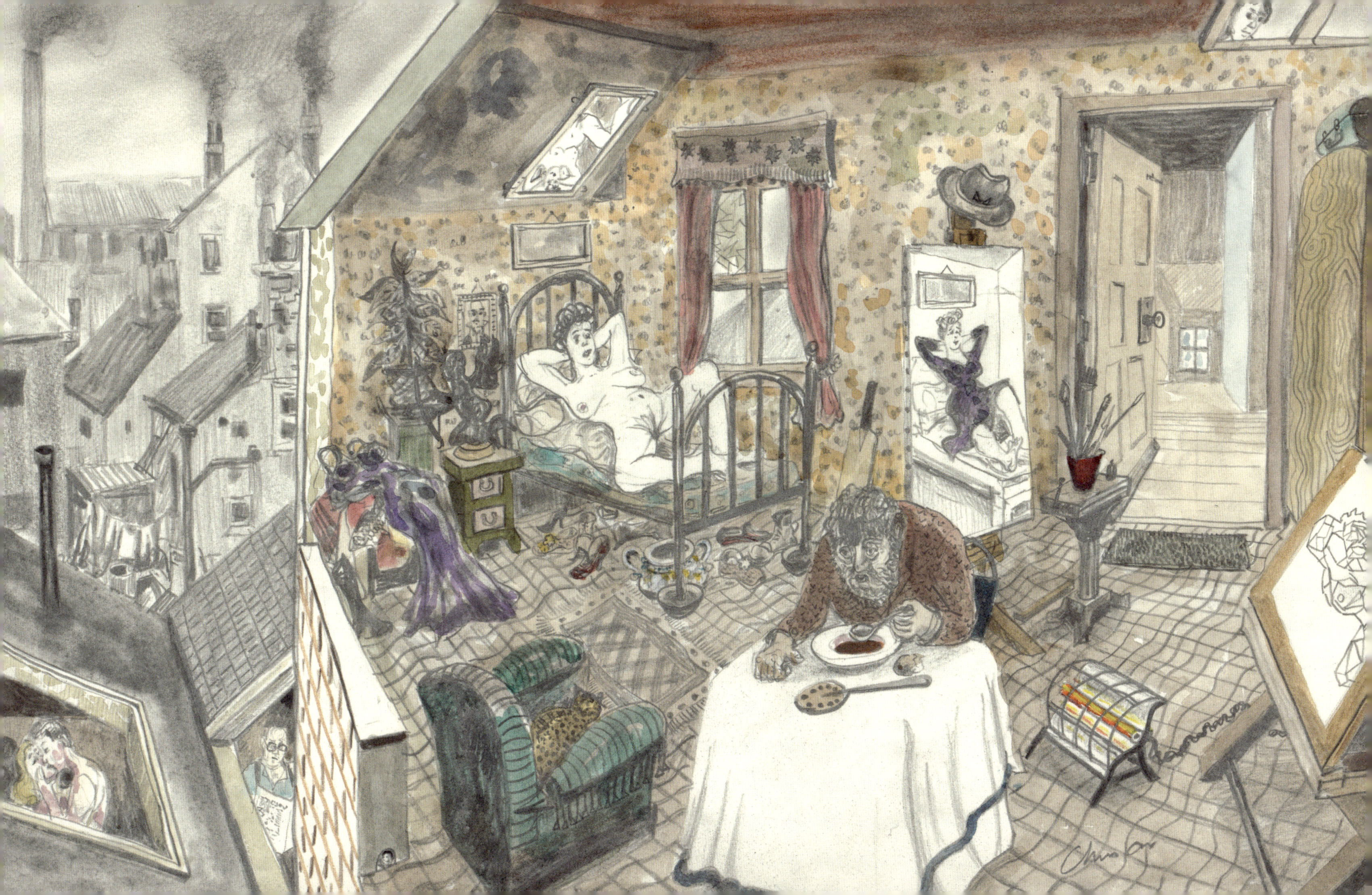

THE FAUVES' PICNIC

Les Fauves 1904-1908

Henri Matisse, Albert Marquet, André Derain, Raoul Dufy painters

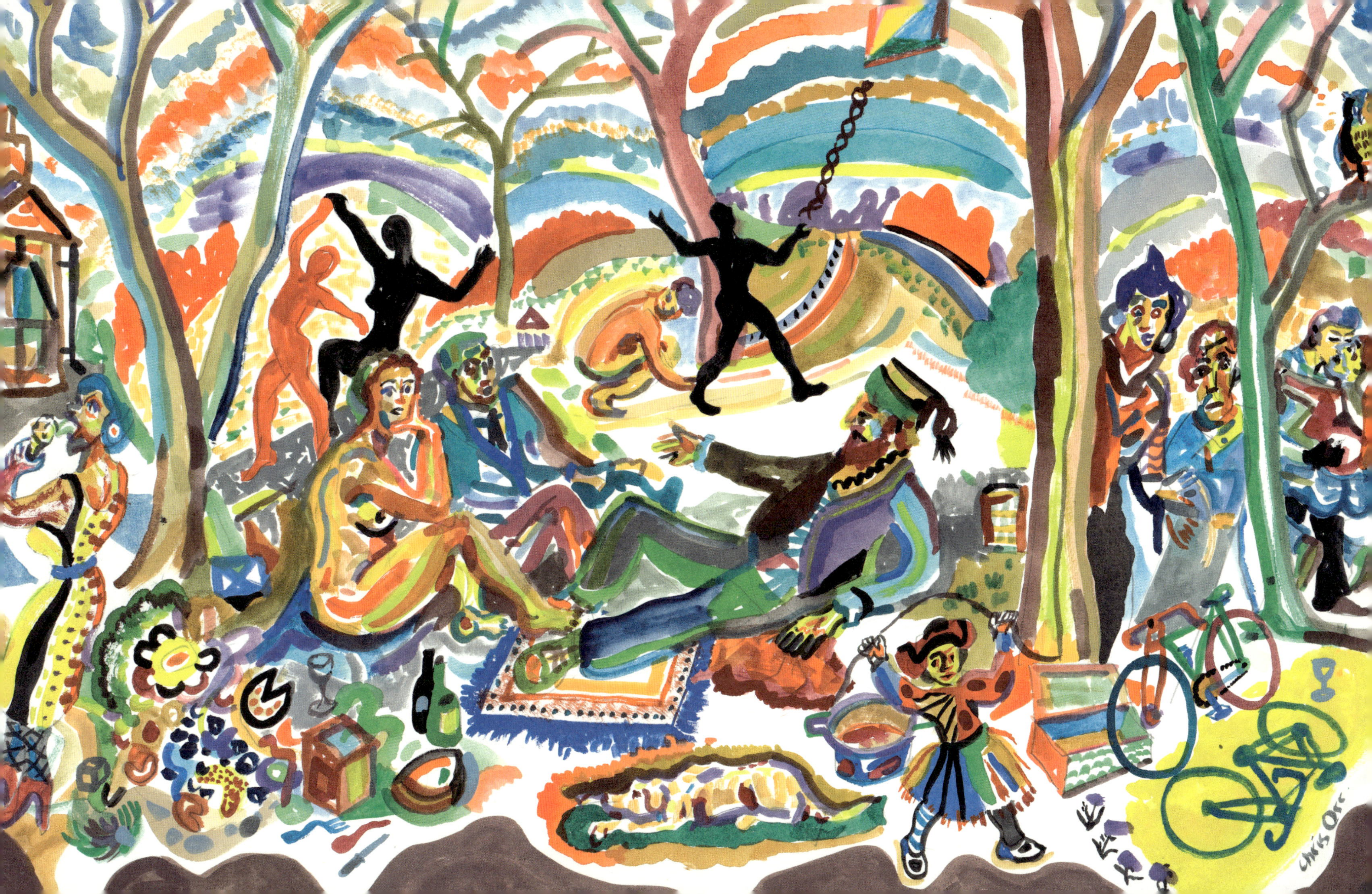
chris Orr

An Indian Miniaturist enjoys the heat

Bengal School 19th & 20th century painters

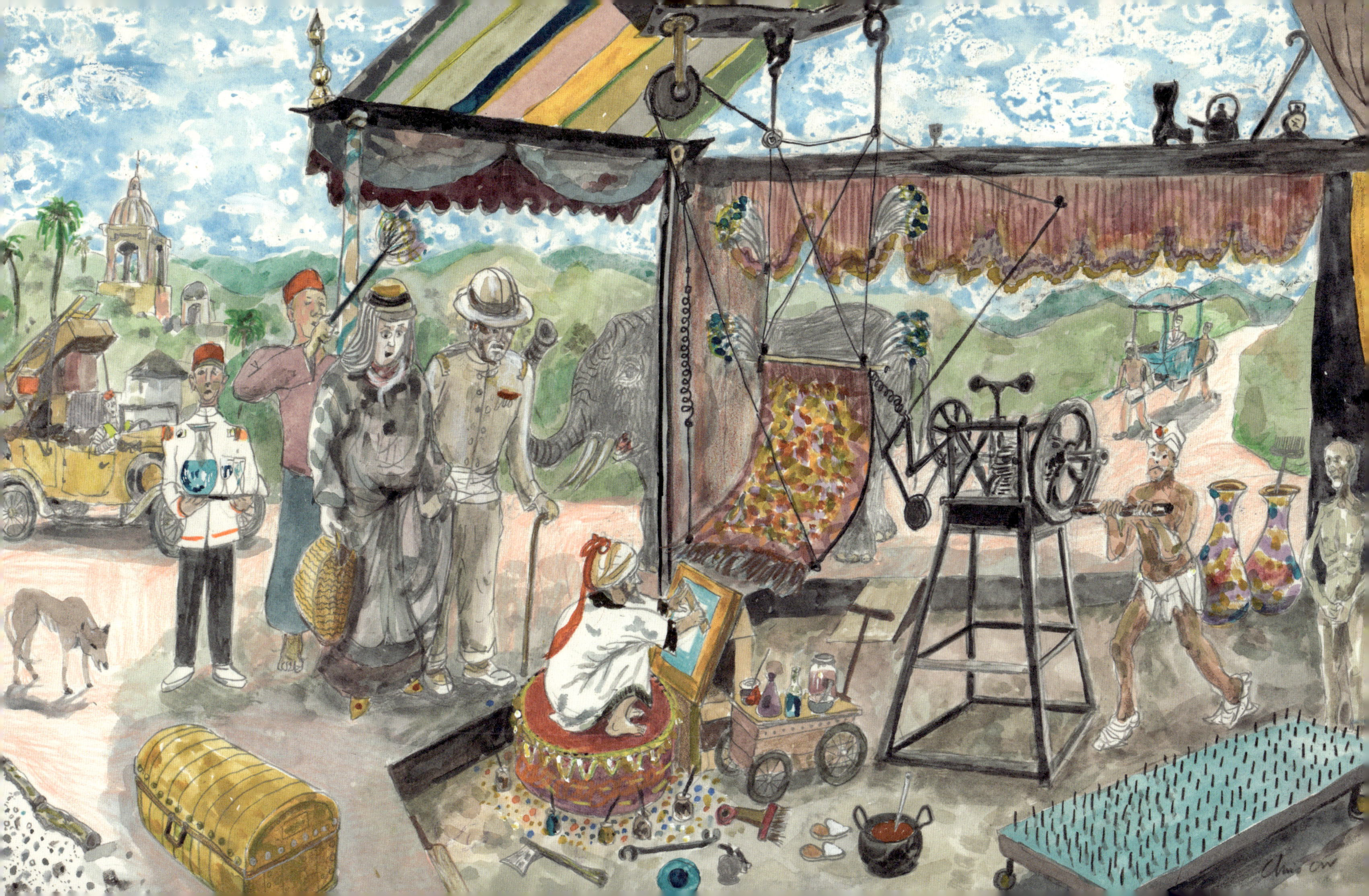

The Divine Comedy —
Reginald Marsh at Coney Island

Reginald Marsh, painter 1898-1954

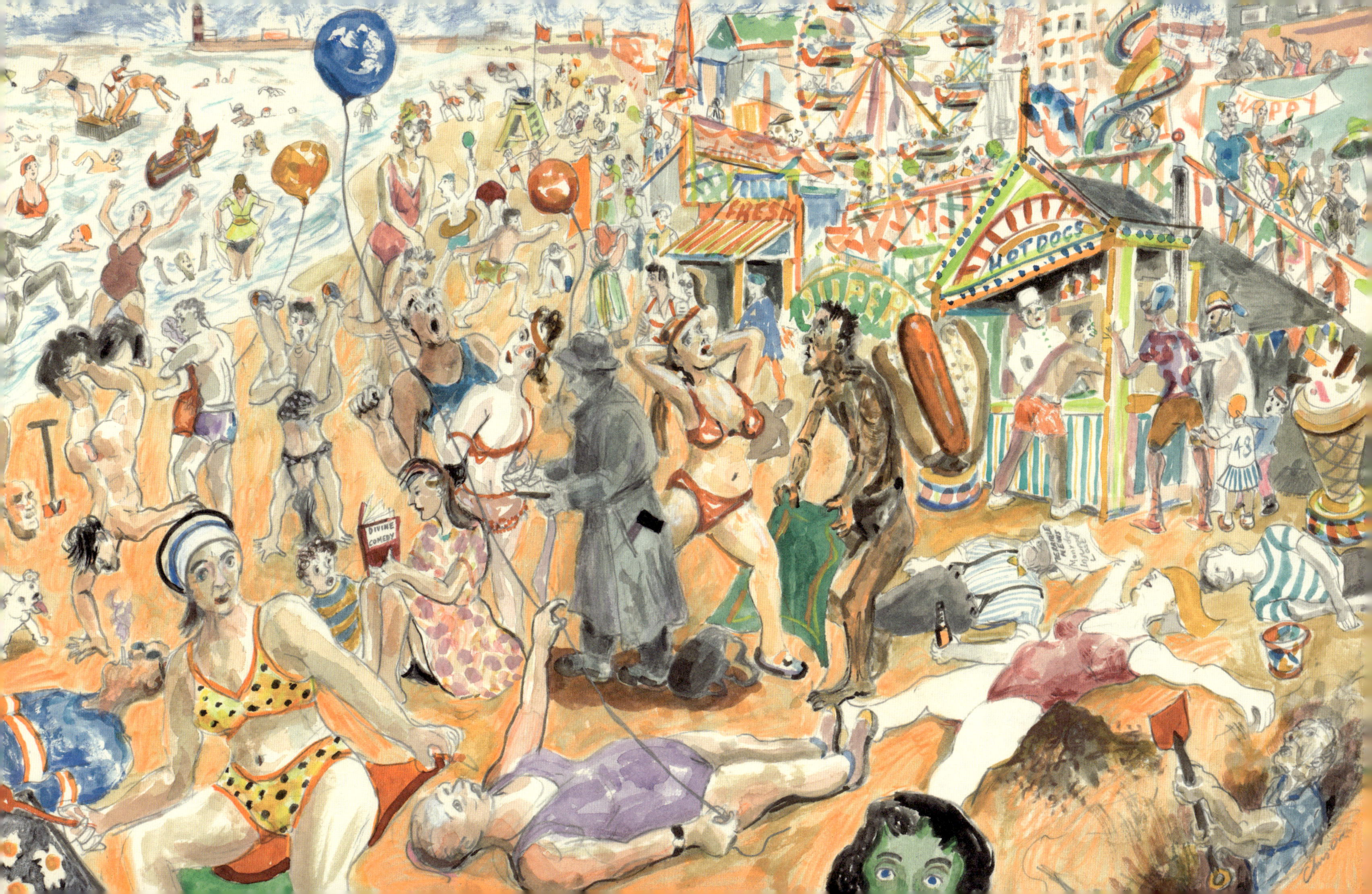
HAPPY
FRESH
HOT DOGS
DIVINE COMEDY
48

Hokusai's troublesome umbrella

Katsushika Hokusai, painter 1760-1849

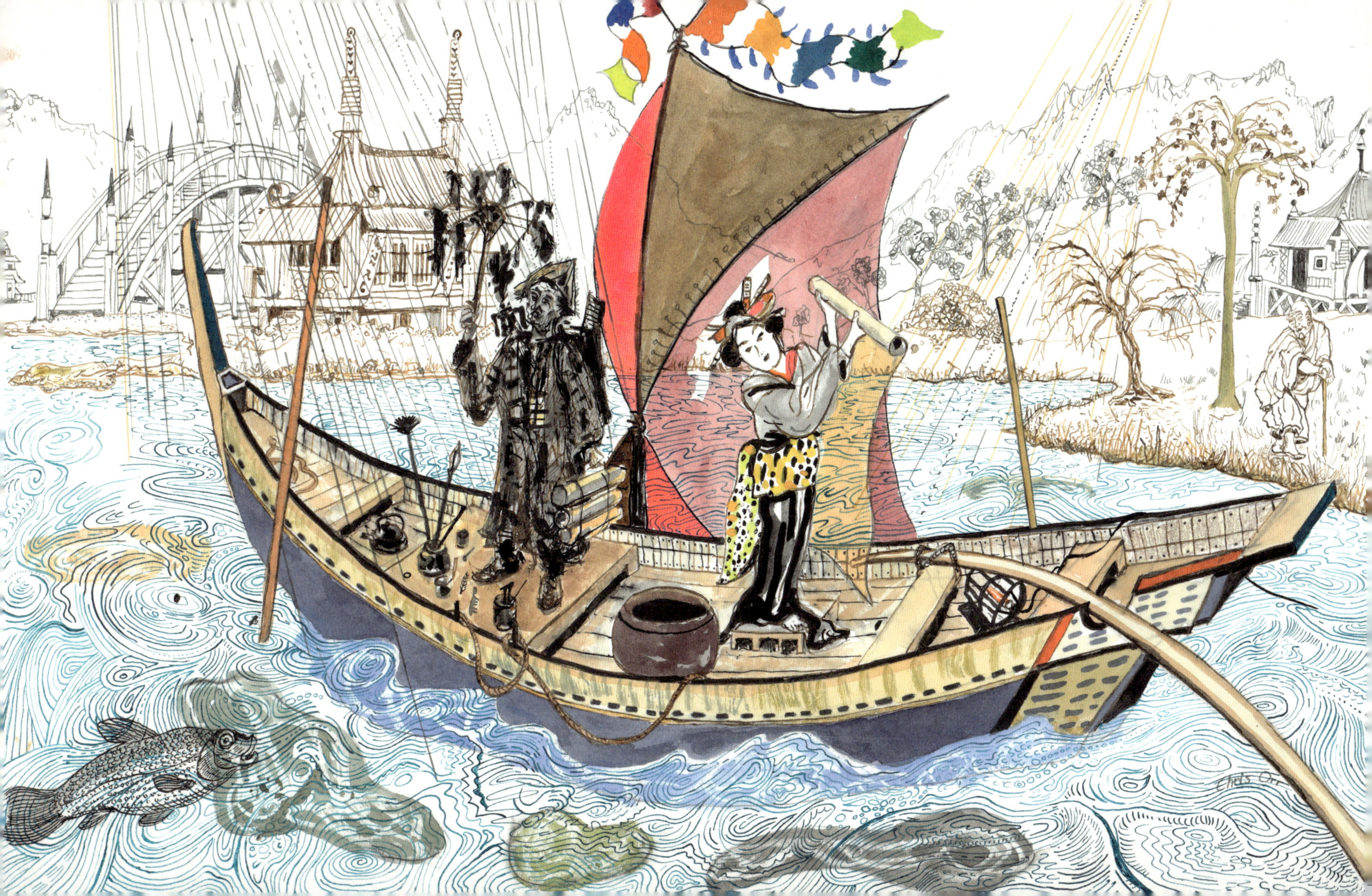
Chris Orr

Louise Bourgeois was awfully fond of toast

Louise Joséphine Bourgeois, sculptor 1911–2010

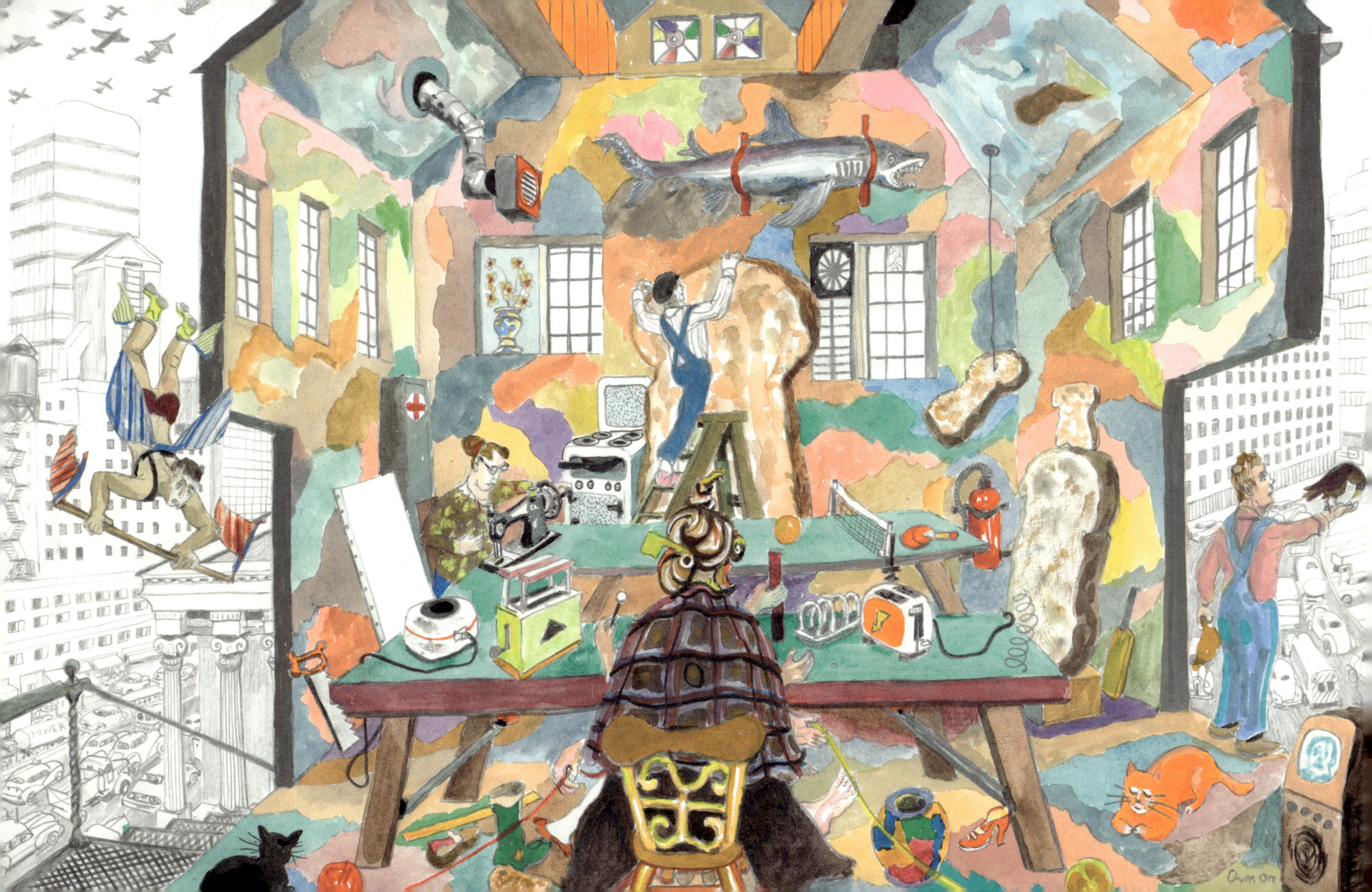
POWER

Canny Thomas Bewick by the banks of the Tyne

Thomas Bewick, engraver 1753-1828

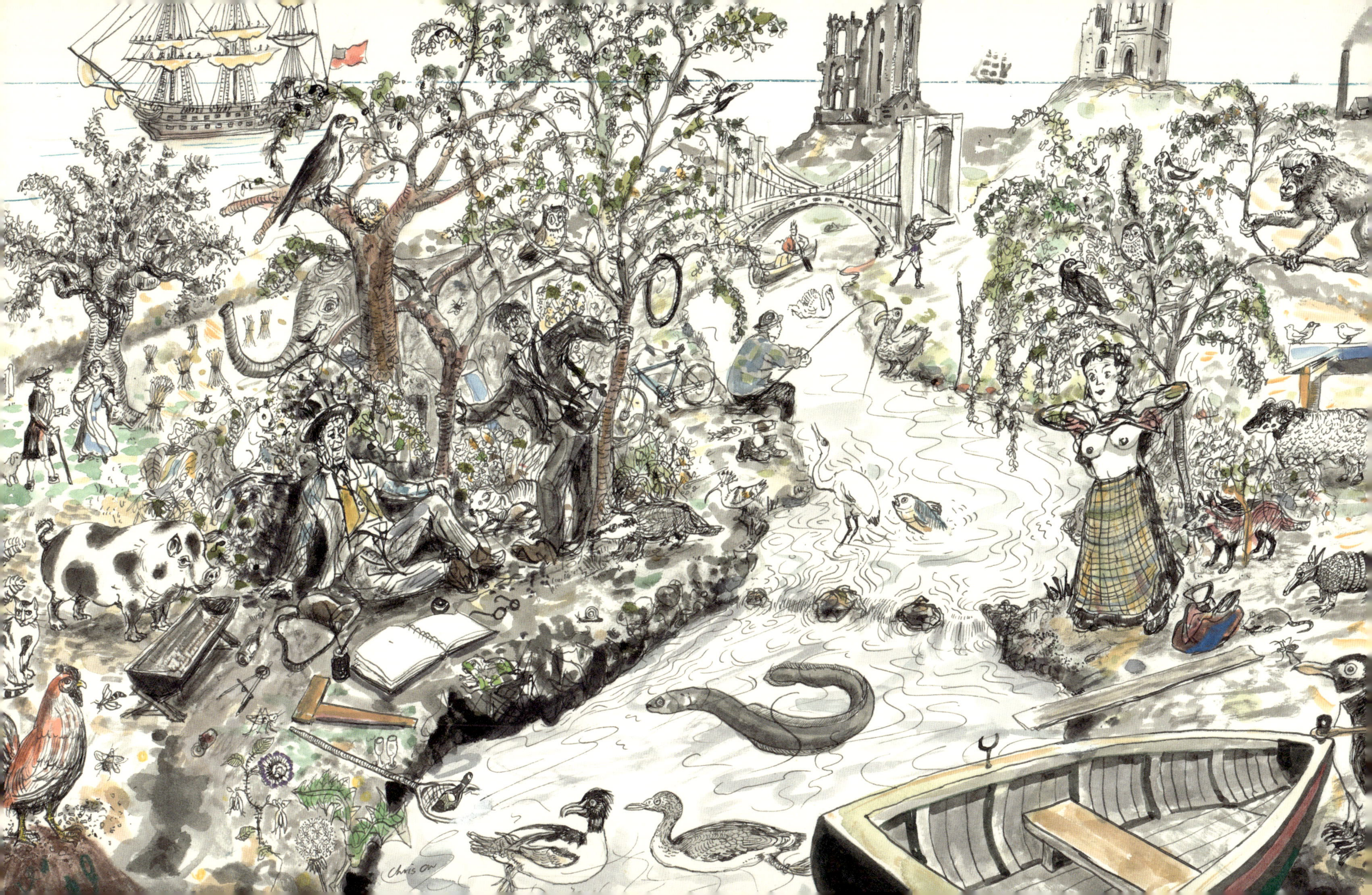
Chris Orr

A case of Zoomania involving Leonora Carrington

Leonora Carrington, painter/writer 1917-2011

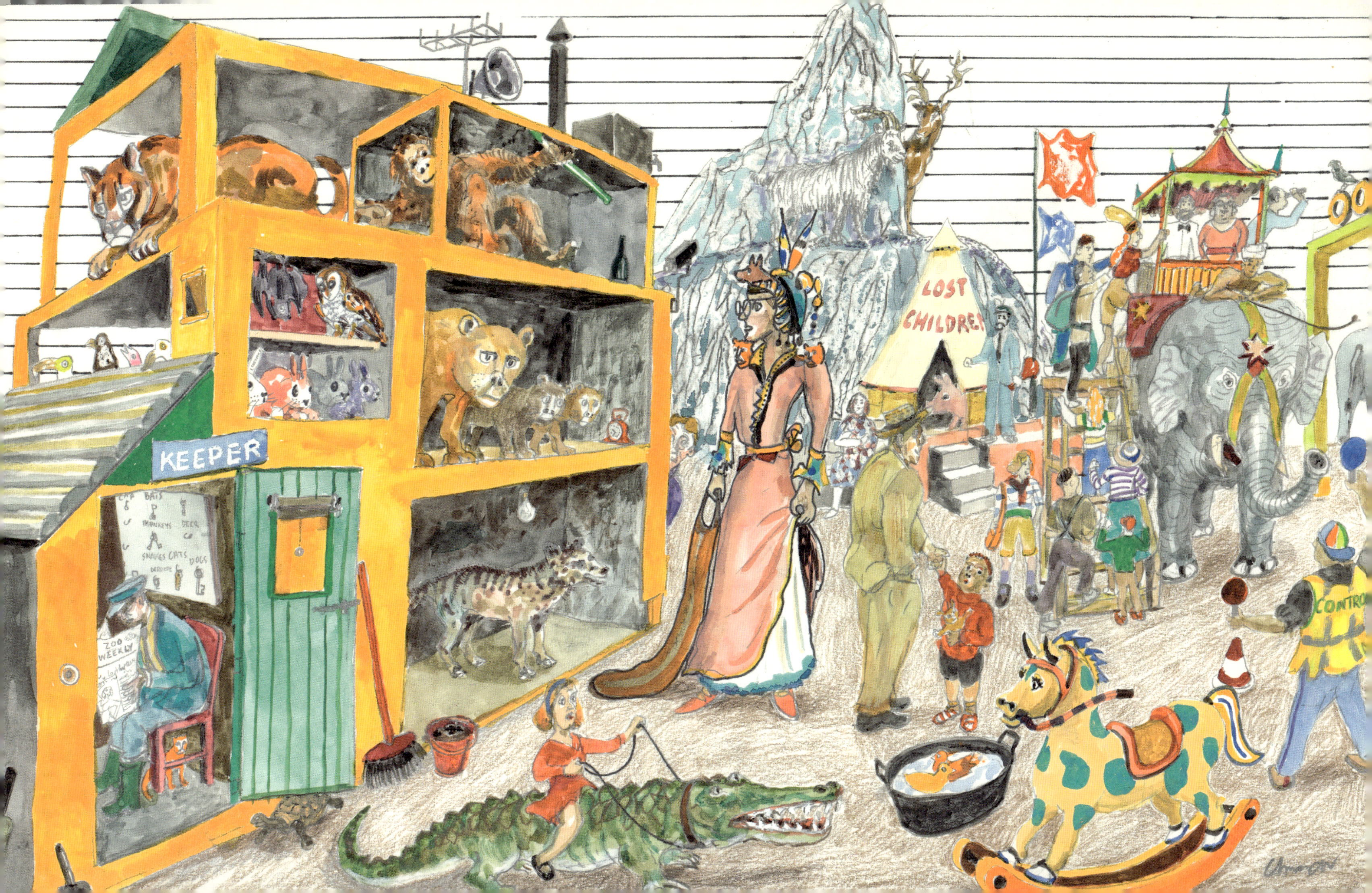
KEEPER
BATS
MONKEYS
DEER
SNAKES
CATS
DOGS
ZOO WEEKLY
LOST
CHILDRE

Things that go bump in the night
Rembrandt's Haunted House

Rembrandt Harmenszoon van Rijn, painter 1606 - 1669

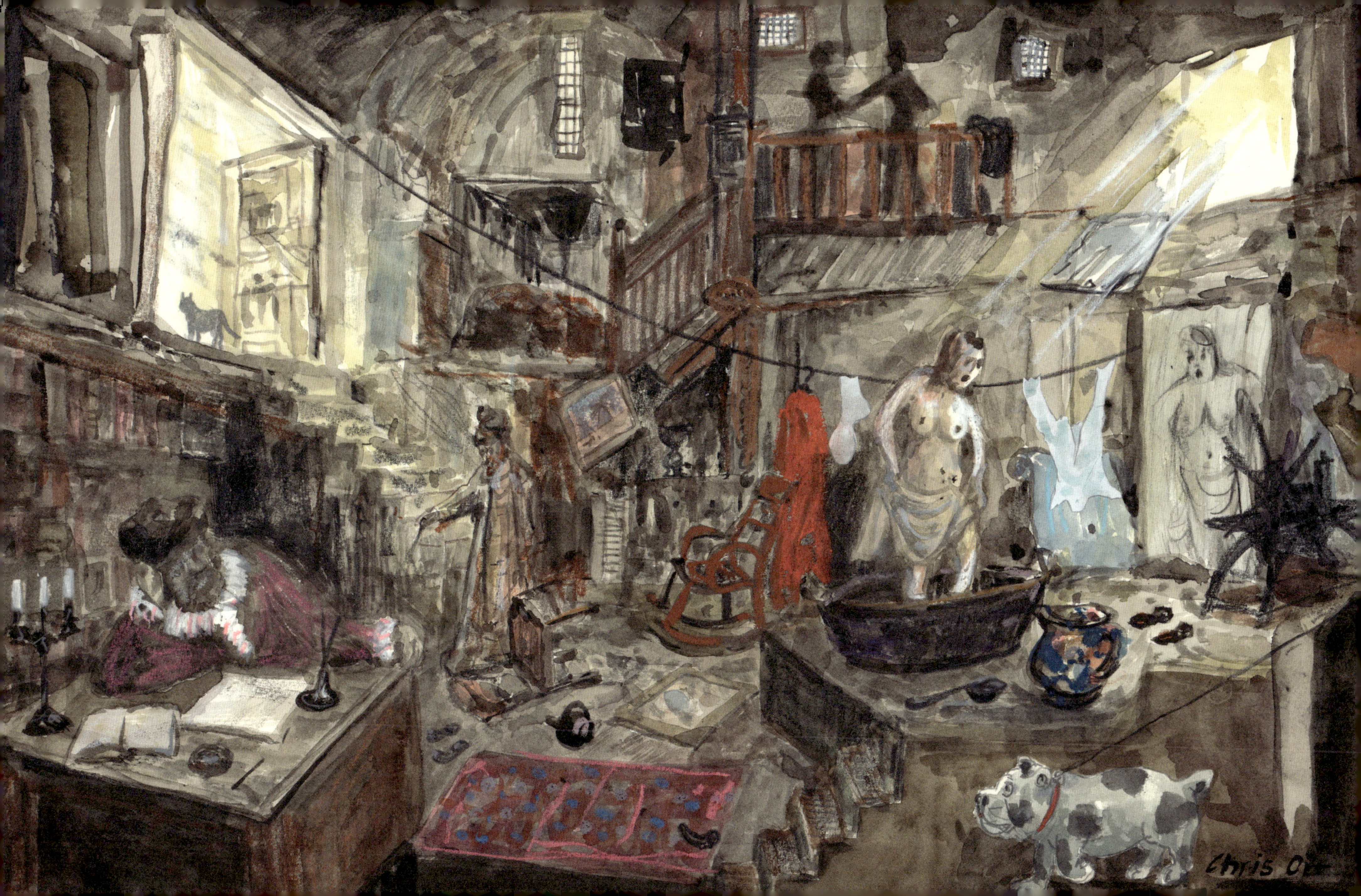
Chris Orr

Donald McGill
Up before the Beak again

Donald Fraser Gould McGill, postcard artist 1875–1962

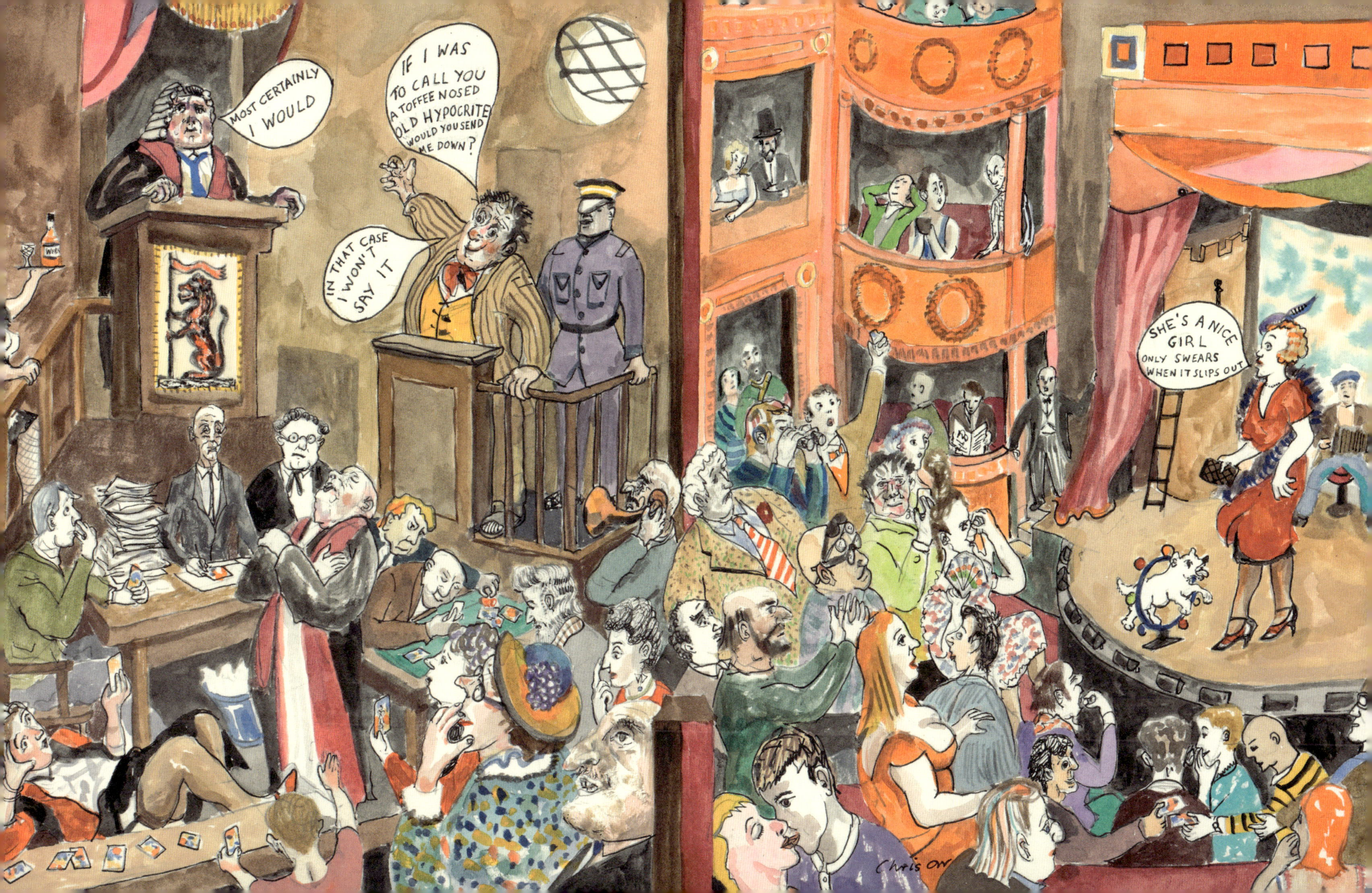

IF I WAS TO CALL YOU A TOFFEE NOSED OLD HYPOCRITE WOULD YOU SEND ME DOWN?
MOST CERTAINLY I WOULD
IN THAT CASE I WON'T SAY IT
SHE'S A NICE GIRL ONLY SWEARS WHEN IT SLIPS OUT

A Sculptor in the Valley of the Kings makes a mistake

16th - 11th century BC

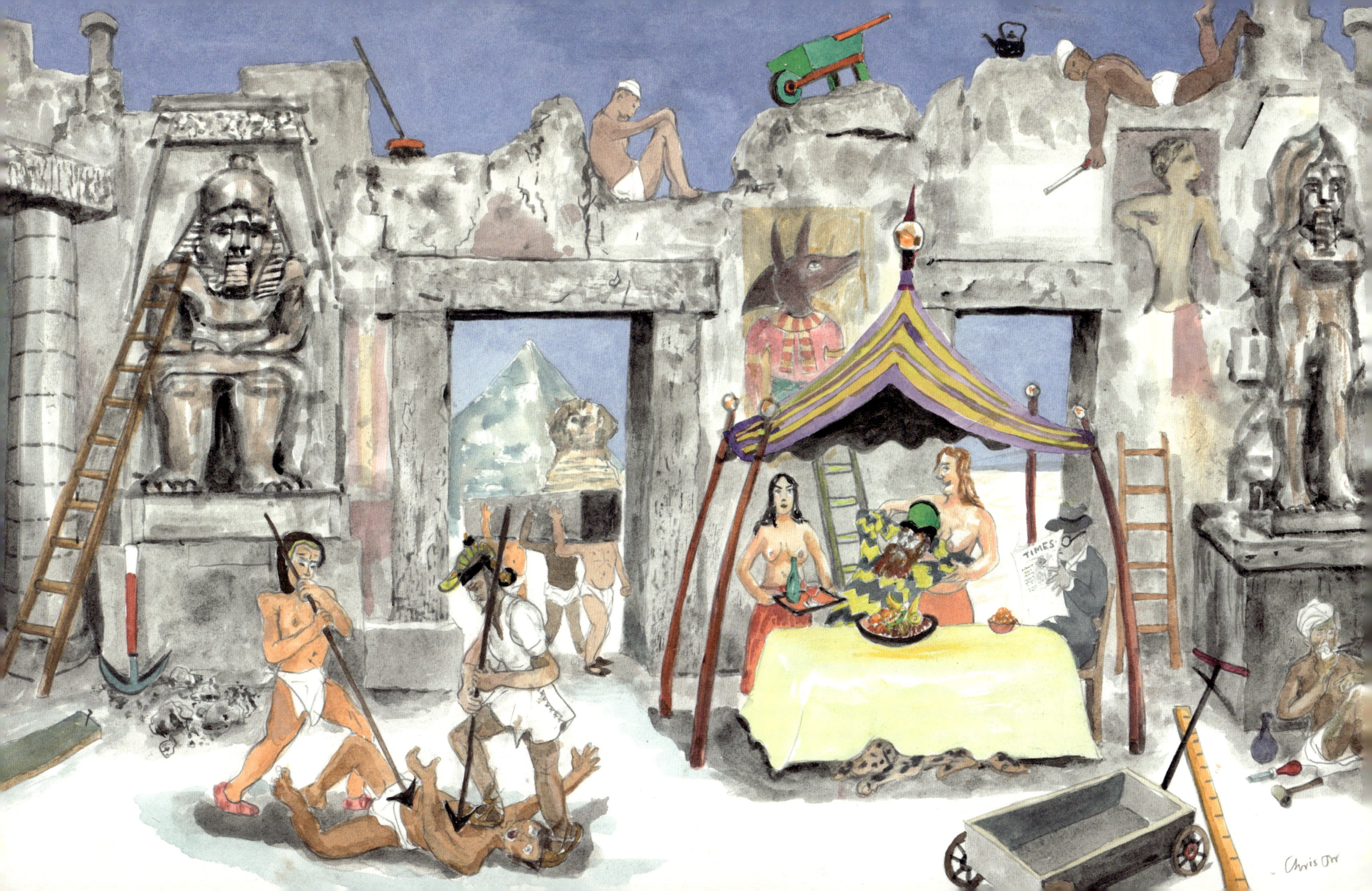

TIMES
Chris Orr

The discomfort of Charles Rennie Mackintosh

Charles Rennie Mackintosh 1868-1928

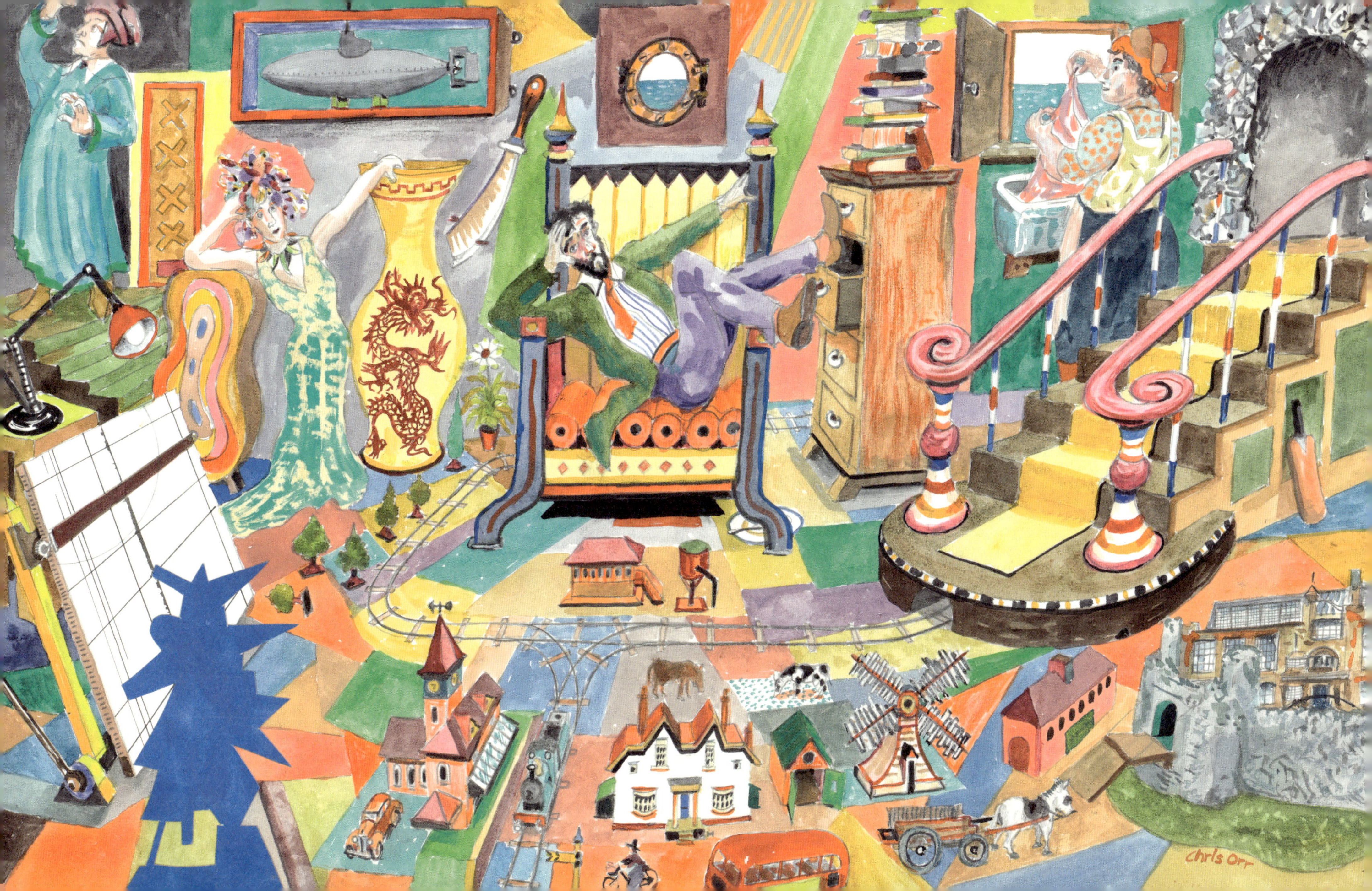
Chris Orr

Brief Encounter
L.S. Lowry meets Beryl Cook

Laurence Stephen Lowry RA 1887 – 1976 painters
Beryl Cook 1926 – 2008

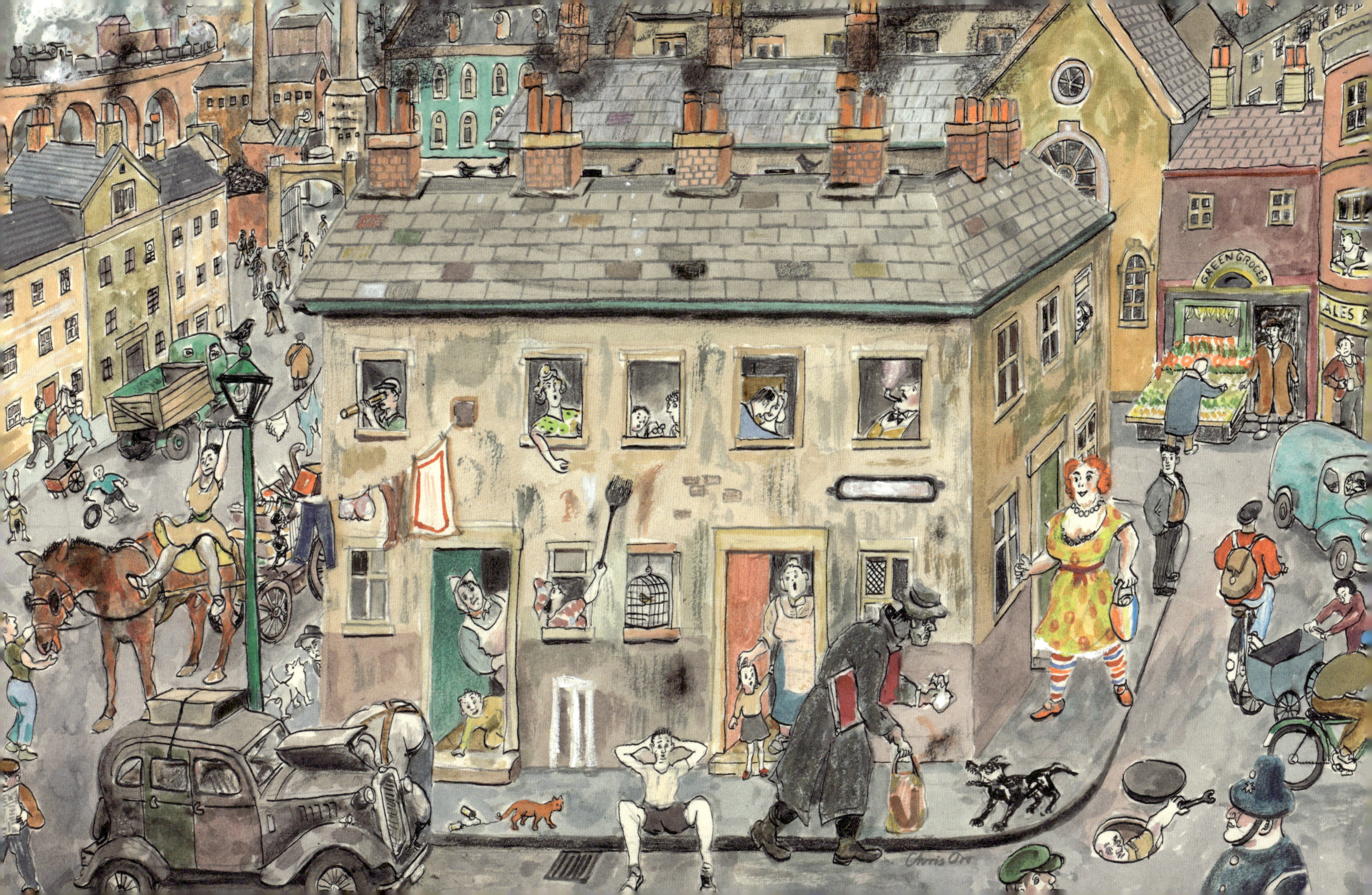
GREENGROCER
ALES
Chris Orr

Hieronymus Bosch — Time Traveller

Jheronimus van Aken, Hieronymus Bosch, painter 1450–1516

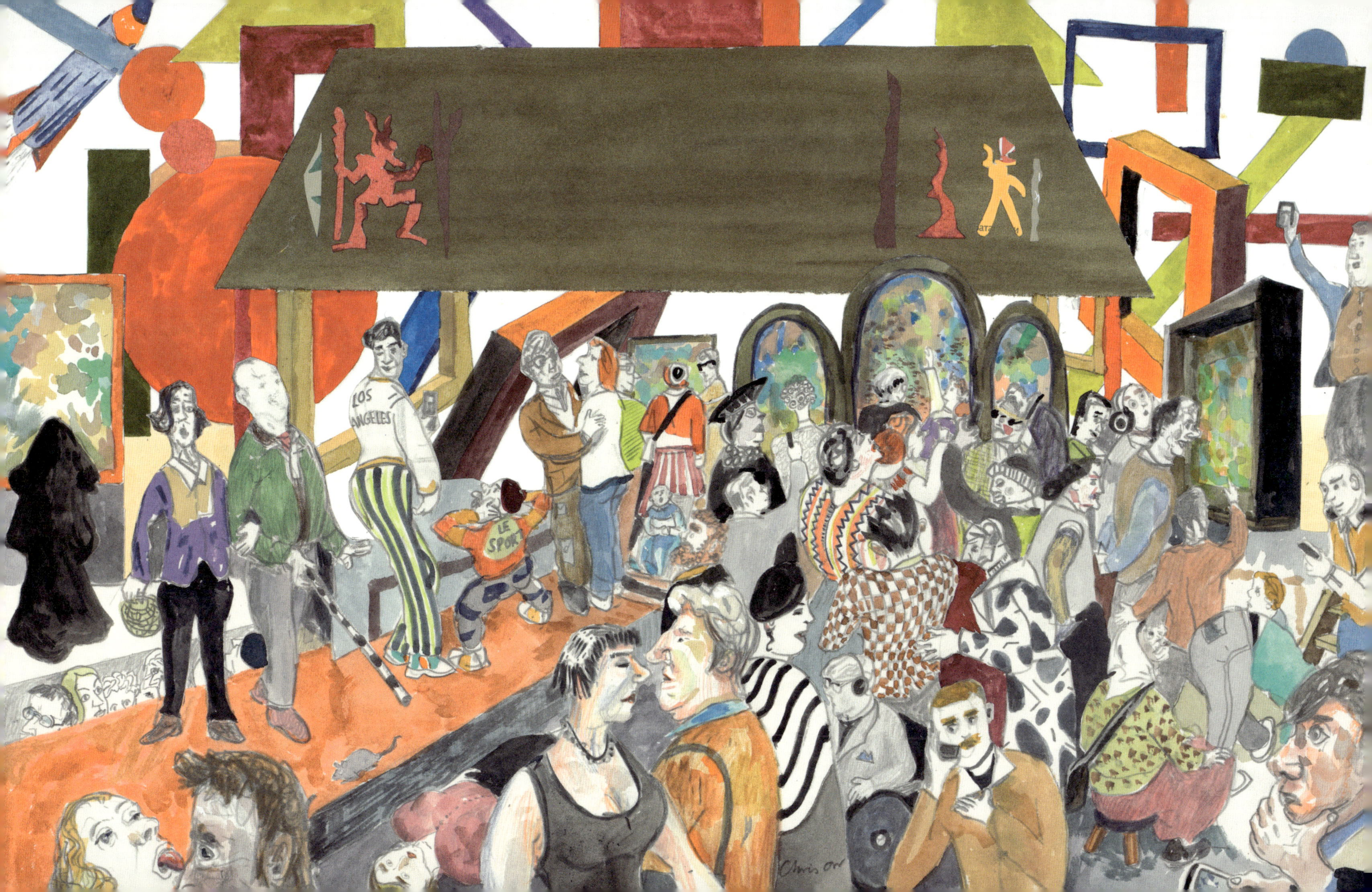
LOS ANGELES
LE SPORT
Chris Orr

Goya in Bordeaux

1746 - 1828

Francisco José de Goya y Lucientes painter & printmaker

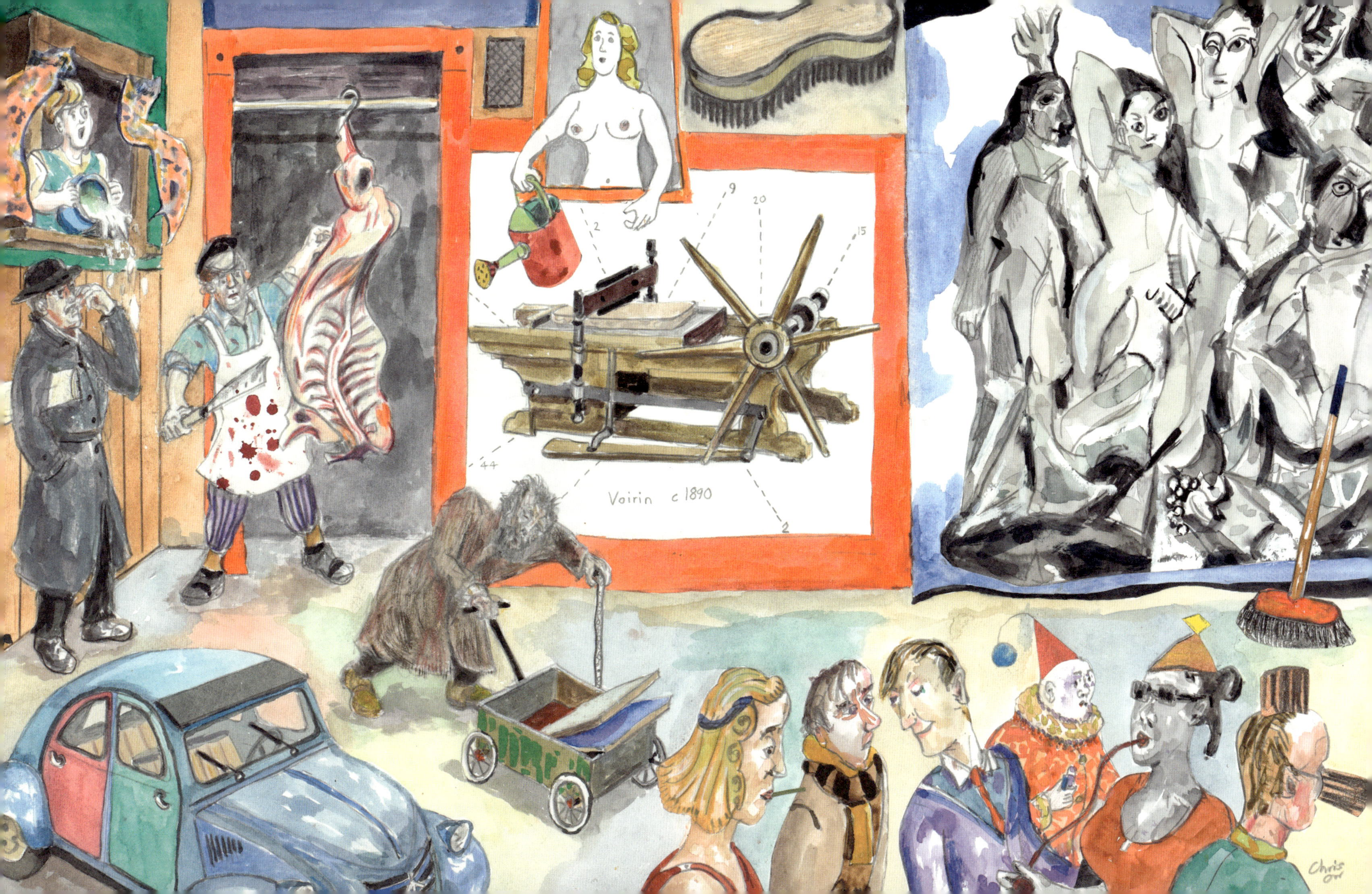
2
9
20
15
44
Voirin c 1890
2
Chris Orr

A TOUR OF THE CAGES

Chris Orr speculates on the inhabitants of his private imaginary zoo

1

VINCENT'S BATTLE WITH COLOUR

This was originally entitled 'Twenty minutes with Vincent would be OK, so long as you had a cast-iron get-out clause'. I imagined him as a somewhat difficult man to get away from. My first drawing featured a visitor in Vincent's studio getting the pre-arranged phone call in order to make an escape. The colour question began to be more important as I worked. Who would imagine Van Gogh with a monochrome affliction? There is an unfortunate condition where, no matter how hard the individual tries, everything goes wrong. I experienced this in my very brief secondary school teaching experience when I had one pupil who, whatever colour he started painting with, could not help himself turning the whole picture black. My Van Gogh cannot get the colour on the canvas. The dog has a particularly bad time.

I love all my Fabulous Artists, even though I take their names in vain, but I was in the wilderness for a number of years with my attitude to Vincent. The bizarre monetary values put on paintings like *Sunflowers* (£62.8 million) so antagonised me that I rejected the man. It was the Royal Academy's exhibition 'The Real Van Gogh: The Artist and His Letters' in 2011 that made me realise my mistake. The relationship between writing and drawing especially enthrals me. I had first considered this idea when I went to China and I began to employ a more calligraphic drawing style. The act of drawing is almost verbal. Each mark is a sound, making a word that stands for a visual point. Van Gogh's *Landscape near Montmajour with a Train* is both an essay and a drawing; a linear space with no space; a continuum of marks that expresses a landscape without ever pretending anything else.

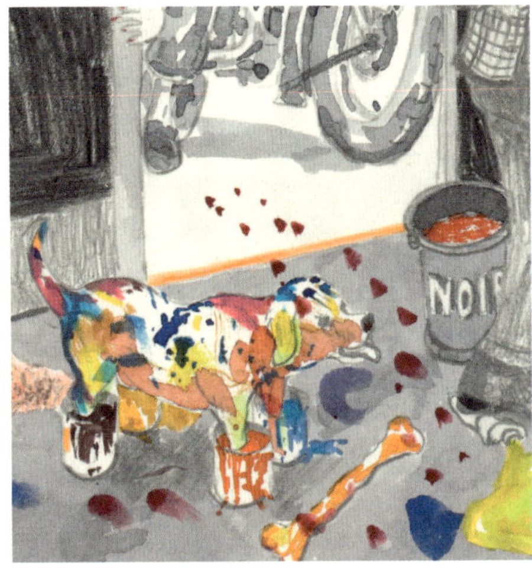

However, the film *Lust for Life* or the song 'Vincent (Starry starry night)' by Don McLean are the way most people see the artist, an unstable tortured genius for whom we should feel pity, fear and reverence. Has there ever been a film about an artist that does any justice to the subject? The real misery of the artist's job is the tedium of application. Day after day they must grind on. Repeated trial and error is an unappealing subject for filmmakers. My Vincent is in a bit of difficulty, but he will win the battle with colour and get it to reside where it belongs. So despite the millions of dollars, I now feel a kinship with him.

2

THE BITS CONSTABLE LEFT OUT

On Thursday 25 May 2017 Kate and I got up at 5 am, made the classic squashy egg sandwiches (boiled eggs, spring onions, garlic, mayonnaise, salt and pepper on sourdough) and beetled off across London on a beautiful summer's morning to visit Constable Country. Even in the early hours London was choked with traffic, the fumes intensified by the new day's rapidly rising heat.

On the A13, it was a slow drive. There was a long procession of lorries and white vans. Squadrons of cars were shimmering in the exhaust gas. By contrast, when we arrived at East Bergholt it was perfectly still. This morsel of England was preserved like a beetle in resin, or a fruit in aspic. It might be possible to hear the distant hoot of a train or the murmur of road traffic, but at this time the overwhelming sound was of bees and a cuckoo calling. For a moment I thought the cuckoo might be a recording broadcast by the National Trust. The smell was of fresh grass and flowers coming awake. Later in the day the place would be crowded with tourists snapping their own bit of 'heritage', jostling to sniff a bit of the bucolic. Is this what the National Trust time machine is for, to allow us to take a brief respite from the horrors of contemporary life? Willy Lott's House and Flatford Mill are there to tickle your fancy and to tickle your fantasy.

In the *Hay Wain* reproductions and the National Trust mise-en-scène, the chocolate-box image of rural bliss, set in a pre-mechanised age, suggests that though many were ragged and unschooled, they were happy with the simple things. A golden age of ignorant bliss. A sign at Flatford Mill suggests the horse and cart in the painting are fording the river. Surely, they are in the middle of the millpond to water the horse and rest after the back-breaking work of transporting the harvest? Life was not a charming idyll. The honesty of Constable's painting has been reassigned.

Later in the day we visit Harwich, part of the East Coast Brexit Axis. Not far geographically, but a long way metaphorically from East Bergholt. The town has a rather disaffected and sad life on the margins. The container port is busy with the traffic of wealth that passes through but bypasses the locals.

My work from Constable's *Hay Wain*, under the title 'The bits Constable left out', plays with the idea of the artist as both subversive and reactionary. My Constable has a blank canvas in front of him. Willy Lott's house is for sale, the back yard shows sign of occupation by travellers, and red indians are coming downriver. Like all of my miserable artists, Constable is struggling with making something that signifies his experience. Perhaps there is an artist who can paint the pound shops and chippies so that one day they can become part of our national treasure?

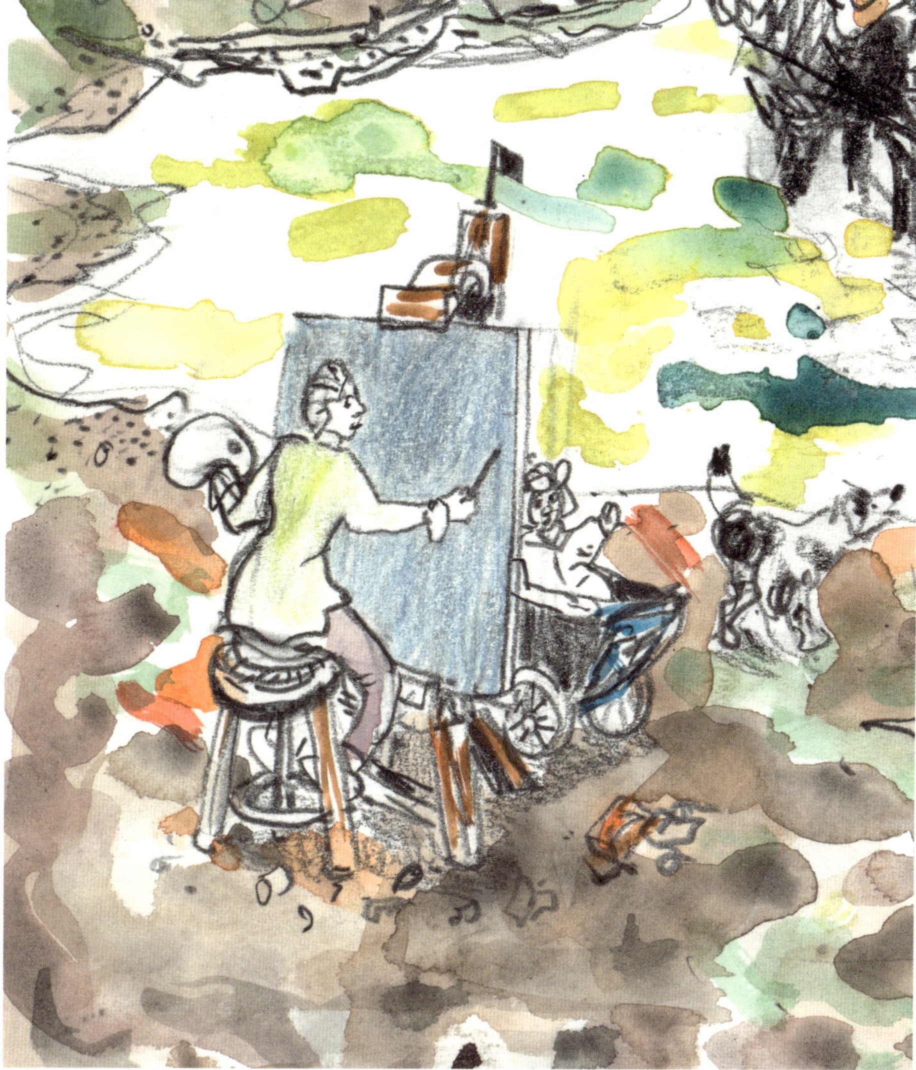

3

FRIDA KAHLO (DIEGO'S DINNER)

When I were a lad, it was axiomatic that when a man came home from work his dinner would be on the table. My father, who was in the printing trade, always looked a bit sheepish when he came home and found a plateful awaiting him. This was probably because he had had a rather good business lunch, washed down with a pint or two, and my mother's offering was frequently a bit below par. Also, he was a keen cook himself and did a mean dripping on toast.

Frida is stirring a very colourful stew, not dissimilar to her painting. She paints with her right hand and cooks with her left. She makes a mess, but only in designated areas. Her cooking instruments (or are they something medical?) include a stirrup pump, hacksaws, pincers, tongs, callipers and a spade. Her cooking is a kind of revenge. The gas cooker is a variant of the examples that appear in my paintings of Louise Bourgeois and Barbara Hepworth. It lurks somewhere inside my mind, the quintessential gas cooker. I am enamoured too, by a one-bar electric fire that appears with Hokusai, Walter Sickert, Atkinson Grimshaw and Joseph Beuys. I am a catalogue of odd things. Just as my repertoire of characters, whether men or women, all resemble me, so too all the objects that populate my interiors have a familiar ring. I can trace many of them back to my first home in Bromley. As with any other catalogue, feel free to cross reference anything in my pages.

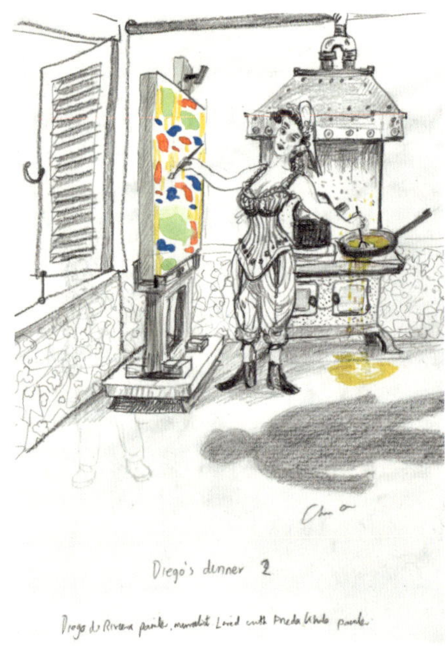

The mariachi band's dog, reminiscent of Nipper the HMV dog, will be welcomed inside for the subsequent picture 'A fry-up for Frida'. Of the band itself, only the guitar and the sombrero will survive.

4

DIEGO RIVERA (A FRY-UP FOR FRIDA)

Husband-and-wife teams are an important subject for me. This picture should be seen in conjunction with 'Diego's dinner'. One strand of wisdom suggests that you should not share your life with another person who does the same job, because rivalry in the professional sphere could sour the domestic life. On the other hand, who but a fellow artist can understand the imperative to 'get on' and try once again to crack the nuts that most artists spend their lives struggling with? Dissatisfaction dogs the artist. Real resolution is difficult and perhaps only retrospectively can an artist's output be judged successful; that means when the artist is dead, so there is a job for all those critics out there after all.

Frida and Diego share the same kitchen, which is also a studio. I have always drawn a close parallel between cooking and making art. Just as even the most delicious meal is consumed and forgotten very quickly, similarly attempts on the canvas are quickly consigned to the bin or the reserve store and once more the artist must start again. Some of the world's greatest paintings hanging in museums today were probably nearly junked. Satisfaction is followed by hunger – even after a feast the next meal beckons. Cooking and painting share the same intuitive element, and no matter how good the recipe, or how accurately it is followed, success comes from something intangible. The combination of intuitive senses, memory and guesswork is vital.

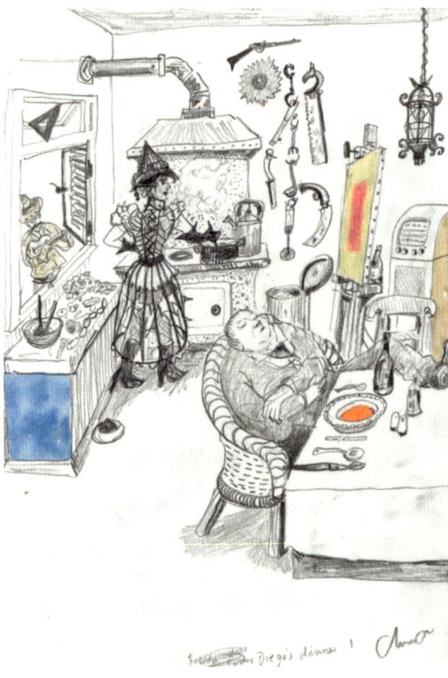

Diego is juggling his eggs. Fried eggs may be his only dish. Poor Frida has to paint in her sleep (probably because she is usually too busy cooking Diego's dinner). Although this is the same kitchen as in 'Diego's dinner', just as our memories play tricks in the recall of things, these interiors may be at once almost the same but completely different. I always loved those puzzle pictures where you had to spot the difference between two apparently identical images.

Is 'A fry-up for Frida' from Diego's point of view, and 'Diego's dinner' from Frida's point of view? Or vice versa? Or neither?

5

SEARCHING FOR A LOST BUTTON AT JACKSON'S

Of all the twentieth-century artists, Jackson Pollock can take first prize for living the legend of his own history. I love the raw energy of his production. There is nothing ironic or humorous in his output, he had to wait for me to give him that twist. In my version he is in a house of paint splashes, drips, daubs and smears; from the kitchen to the dog, everything is covered. Jack the Dripper. Only the canvas on the floor has colour (except for the blue poles outside the front door) but everything else has taken on the black and white splattering. The artwork is not confined to the canvas, it has conquered everything. Woe betide anyone who tries to find a lost button.

The work of an artist does not end at the canvas edge any more than the writer's world is sealed inside their books. Problems arise when the artist spends more time on the public image than the painting. I heard that Joseph Beuys lectured his students on the correct way to behave at a private view, but of course he was being ironic. Pollock's reputation does not seem to be part of any plan but it completely synchronises with the work.

Although it is difficult to find the button, there is an amazing sense of order in Jackson's work that contradicts his critics.

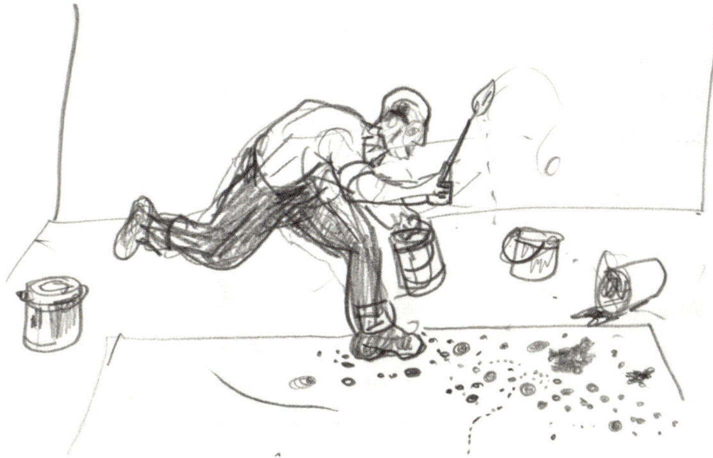

6

ANGELICA KAUFFMAN IS BARRED FROM THE ROYAL ACADEMY LIFE ROOM

The life room, where students draw from the nude model, has been central to art education since time immemorial. We could blame the Ancient Greeks. Angelica Kauffman was one of the founding members of the Royal Academy in 1768. However, it was considered inappropriate for women to take part in life classes. Indeed, up until the late 1930s life drawing was segregated by gender at many institutions. Who knew what might happen if men and women sat alongside each other looking at the naked human form? Since the fundamental training for being a successful painter at the time was study from life, female artists were at a grave disadvantage.

In my first years at art school I drew in the life room for at least two days a week (the model was usually someone the age of my grandmother so there was little risk of going berserk), but the drums of change were sounding. A radical rethink of the importance of life drawing was underway. 'Basic design' was the new thing. Nowadays only those with a declared interest will opt for life drawing as a study programme and generations of graduates have emerged who haven't experienced drawing the figure.

For a few years I helped Bryan Kneale run the drawing studio at the Royal College of Art, where we attempted to revive interest in life drawing, arguing its importance as a humanist study. The studio serviced all the faculties of the college and although we got many enthusiasts from the design departments, the fine artists were notably absent. My method of teaching involved drawing alongside the students as well as talking to them about their efforts, so I got another chance to get deeply involved in life drawing on a regular basis. The study of the human figure seems to me to have been the most central part of my art education.

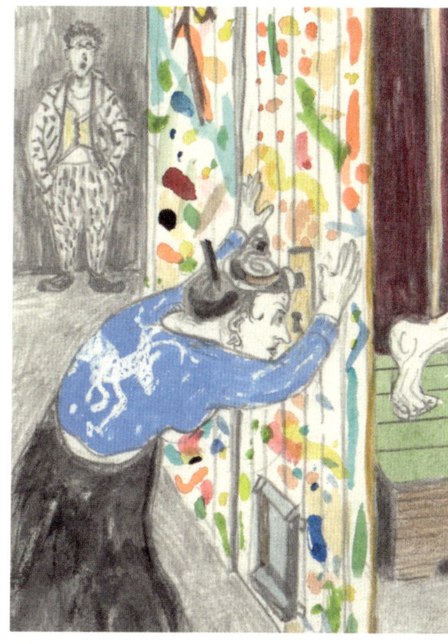

7

PICASSO'S BUSY DAY

Picasso is the impossible genius who overshadows every little whimper made by twentieth-century artists. Prolific, adroit, revolutionary, rich, inspired and ubiquitous – that's the story. Picasso must have had many a busy day.

With a sceptical eye, I examine in the form of a strip cartoon a typical, or not-so-typical, day for our hero. My Picasso is a cross between Tintin and Monsieur Hulot (Jacques Tati's film of his holiday is my all-time favourite) but he does not have such a good time. He fails to get the girls. He decides against the studio and goes to the sea. Rather than having sex in a beach hut, he builds a sandcastle. He drinks alone in a bar. His pottery gets out of control, and he has the wrong colour blanket to distract the raging bull. Of course, he does make it to the bank to pay in his zillions, but when he finally enters the studio, the model has made 'modern art' before he can get started. Picasso's canvas remains blank.

A friend who actually met the great man said that the one thing he noticed about him was that he was very clean. When I quizzed Patrick Heron about Picasso, whom he had met at a conference in Sheffield, he could not come up with one memorable piece of information.

I suspect that he was none of the things we have made him out to be. The critical industry has worked overtime on fleshing out the 'real' Picasso. My small contribution is a little push the other way. He is the artist we would all like to have been, but maybe he never was?

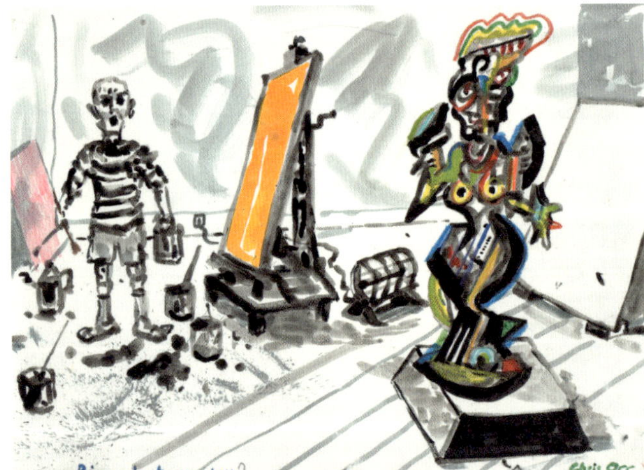

8

ATKINSON GRIMSHAW AT WORK IN TYPICAL CONDITIONS

He painted the newly gas-lit streets of our cities. He liked a bit of moonlight as well. What a revolution the new lighting technology must have been – transforming the dark winter months into a brave new illuminated world. Shopping, courting and going out for the night were revolutionised. I don't think Grimshaw painted Liverpool or Manchester *en plein air*. The paintings have a tranquil, finished and composed studio quality. Did he have artificial light in his studio? Many urban lyricists see beauty in the extremes of the everyday, but often need the calm of private space to achieve it.

I appreciate the comfort of my own workroom, but need and enjoy painting and drawing outside as well. It has some of the qualities of an extreme sport. You must be organised, tenacious and resourceful (ready to compromise). A week I spent in Times Square making a painting was successful despite the endless trails of tourists with useless advice and ill-judged compliments. Snatching short spells of drawing in Beijing and Shanghai before a crowd of overenthusiastic onlookers could assemble was an Olympic sport. Turner extolled the virtues of real experience as a driver of authenticity. Famously he lashed himself to the mast of a boat in a storm to get the genuine experience. Is there any point today? Aren't the super-duper lenses in our cameras and phones more than sufficient? I would argue not. Human perception still manages to have more going for it as a multi-sensory route. You must smell what you are looking at.

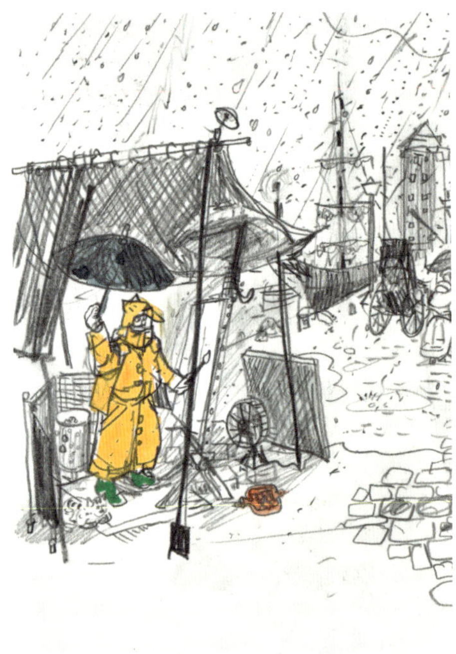

Even if Grimshaw didn't do much *in situ* I have dumped him back in the environment. He is very cosy though, with a hot water bottle, electric fire, all-weather gear, possibly a hip flask and a bivouac. He will not be troubled by the ladies of the night.

9

DAME LAURA KNIGHT SHOPLIFTING IN HARRODS

It's not true! She is only filching an idea! In her painting of herself, clothed, with a nude model, Laura Knight broke new ground, suggesting that the artist was not just the voyeur, but the model as well. I fantasise that she got the idea while walking around a department store, when she glimpsed somebody not dissimilar to herself in a changing room.

That now-rare institution the department store was once as common as the supermarket is today. When I was a boy, it was our treat to go to Medhurst's in Bromley. Apocryphally, H. G. Wells once worked there and reflected the experience in his novel *The History of Mr Polly*. After an afternoon in the department store the cornucopia of things on offer meant you rarely came away empty-handed, even if it was only with a memory or a glimpse of something shocking. The store is a palace of dreams, both erotic and mundane. For me it presents, like illustrated catalogues, a plethora of suggestions all equally capable of development. A theatre of life, from which I can extract what I want.

Shockingly, when Dame Laura was made a Royal Academician in 1936 she was only the third woman to be elected to that august body after Angelica Kauffman and Mary Moser, who had been founder members back in 1768. Dame Laura's paintings betray little reference to what was happening in the rest of the art world in the twentieth century. The English, as a nation of shopkeepers, like their art to be sensible and carefully corralled into recognisable territory. Many other Royal

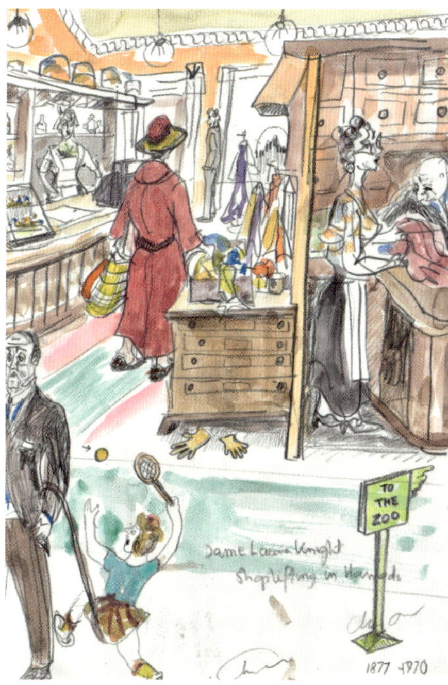

Academicians of the twentieth century kept faith with an English definition of art that substantially ignored the other agendas and concentrated on a more romantic and insular approach.

10

MUNCH ON HOLIDAY

Artists don't take holidays. Like priests, they are on duty all the time, or as my daughter Sally says: artists are on one long holiday and any sense of duty is a figment of their imagination. My Edvard Munch is at the seaside, but next to an out-of-control Punch and Judy on a very rocky outcrop near a whaling station. There may be somebody screaming on the bridge. Don't buy an ice cream here! The easel is on its side. Like most of my poor miserable artists, Munch has nothing on the canvas.

A few years ago I went to an auction of prints at Bonhams in Bond Street, interested in a small signed etching by Munch. It needed some conservation, but I believed it might be a good use of some spare cash I had at the time. Of course, it went for more than three times the reserve price. Out of my league, but it got me into making an etching of my own that had Munch standing in a similar pose on a rocky outcrop with a woman. I introduced the idea that she is scratching her bum like the tennis girl on the Athena poster that adorned many student rooms. This may be the germ of the idea that resulted in the *Miserable Lives*.

I admire Munch's lithographs. Of all artists who have embraced this challenging medium, he takes a uniquely liberated approach, capitalising on the fluid painterly opportunities that the process presents.

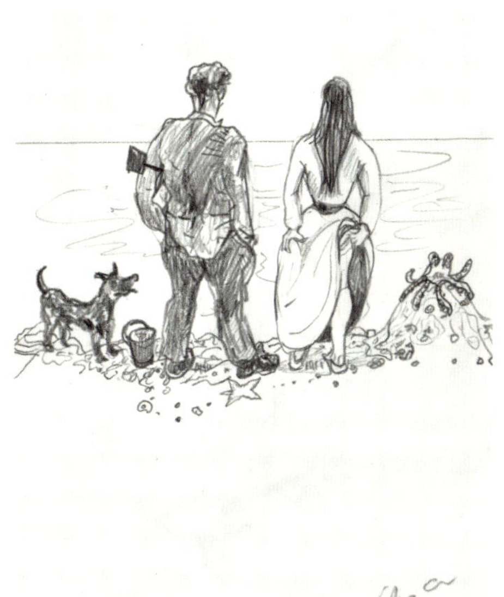

11

MR AND MRS HOPPER AT WORK

A recent cartoon has Donald Trump sitting in the Nighthawks diner on his own, declaring that the place is packed full. Absence is a poignant subject. My picture deals with the thorny question of the influence of artists' partners. I heard that Mrs Hopper, an accomplished painter, had a large influence over her husband, dictating subjects and important details. It is true that, despite art's solitary nature, no painter works alone. The artist always depends on others for nurture, support, inspiration and to do some of the donkey work. The person I always think is absent in a Hopper painting is the painter himself. He is a distant voyeur. Mrs Hopper is present as director, model and stage manager, but he is the patient craftsman who keeps his own presence low key.

The image of the Nighthawks is one of America's most poignant visual exports. It speaks to loneliness and desire, the stillness of the small hours. People of all kinds respond to its emotion. I can almost imagine Osama Bin Laden having a badly reproduced copy sellotaped to his wall. My version, however, returns the subject to the complexity of relationships, within which are tangled responsibilities, causes and effects. No wonder the cat is looking in with bewilderment. My diner has the 'closed' sign up. The inhabitants should go home.

Curiously, loneliness has an attraction, a noble privacy, a heroic battle with the vastness of experience. Forget sweet self-indulgent loneliness. We are all fundamentally alone anyway.

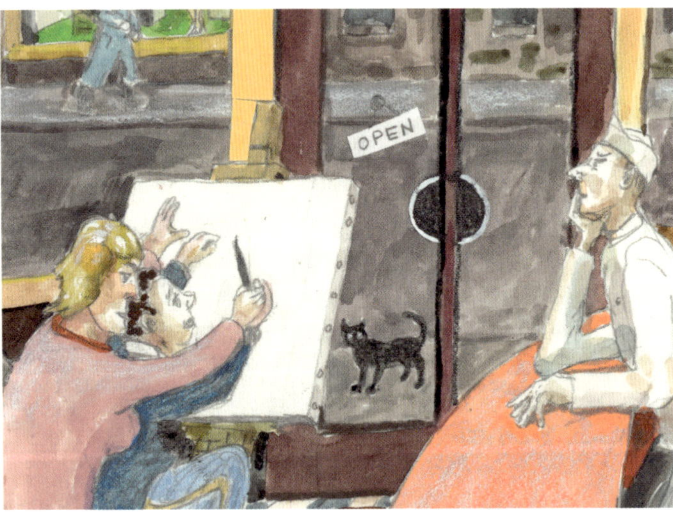

12

FOOT IN THE MOUTH – JAMES GILLRAY

The catalogue for the Gillray exhibition at Tate Britain in 2001 was rather sniffy about some much freer drawings he made towards the end of his life, suggesting they were the product of a deranged mind. In fact, all of his prints and drawings have a manic quality to them, skirting and flirting with excess and debauchery. This is what I love about them. We cannot be sure what Gillray was like as a person, whether he was an absolute stinker (influenced by his strict Moravian upbringing and eighteenth-century London's febrile political and social life) or all sweetness and light from the tides of Enlightenment flooding the city at the time, but I am sure that of all my artists he most firmly straddles the spectrum from miserable to fabulous. The dark cunning of his etched line runs riot through extremes of virtue and dishonour. He was both a paid character-assassin and a free thinker.

Etching involves using acid to make copper plates with recessed lines that can be printed in multiple on paper. Engraving is the cutting of lines into plates. The etching studio is the nearest thing to the alchemist's workshop, with its chemicals and fire, oil and water, solvents and abrasives.

Foot in his mouth, I picture Gillray beside his etching press. He has one leg in a bath of ferric chloride, used to etch the lines into the plates. Miss Humphrey, his companion and publisher, looks on. Napoleon stares down from a drawing on the wall. Around Gillray are the artefacts he used in his prints – the big yellow chest belonging to the Old Lady of Threadneedle Street, the rush crib and Britannia's shield.

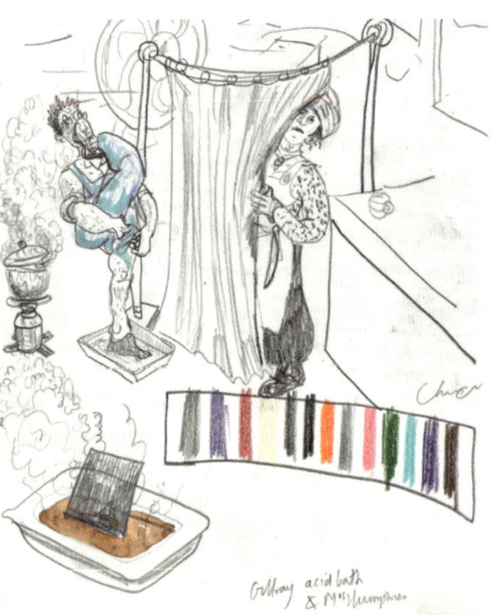

Gillray studied drawing at the Royal Academy Schools; other alumni include William Blake, Constable and Turner. (The furniture in the current Life Room is still the original from the eighteenth century.) Gillray wanted desperately to be taken as a serious painter, but in the cut-throat world of art, he had to make a living, and started to make satirical prints that turned out to be wildly successful. No doubt he harboured the notion that one day he would put all that behind him and be taken as a 'proper' artist. I, too, have been dogged by a dismissive comic label, but there is only one artist in me and that's the one you see before you.

13

DON'T WORRY LADIES AND GENTLEMEN, JOSEPH BEUYS HAS THE COYOTES PERFECTLY UNDER CONTROL

In 1967 I went to Hamburg to visit my friend Konrad Schultz, a fellow student from the Royal College of Art. I was impressed by a Joseph Beuys sculpture show I saw there. It had a lot of grease-and-felt pieces. Elemental sculpture like this was unknown to me. A sculpture, I thought, was an object sitting in space, not an oozing glacier of fat. Furthermore, Beuys indulged in 'actions', recorded in atmospheric grainy films and black-and-white photographs. There was a legendary event with a coyote. I believe no animals were harmed in these performances. What intrigued me was the audience. When they appear in the records it is obvious that they have prepared themselves by looking and wearing something 'cool'. Nobody at a performance wants to appear like an idiot. They must be part of the whole thing, both critical and decorative. So in my picture, more than half the interest is in the audience, ranged up in church-like pews, who are dealing with each other, largely ignoring Beuys and the coyotes. All my spectators at the Beuys event are putting on a performance. The coyotes look pretty tame, but the audience is fierce.

In the bottom left-hand corner is a lifebelt from the *Wilhelm Gustloff* – a relic from the greatest ever sea disaster, which few people in England know about. During this, over 9,000 Germans, mainly women and children, were drowned escaping Gdynia on a Nazi cruise ship at the end of the Second World War. I learnt about it from Gunter Grass in his novel *Peeling the Onion*.

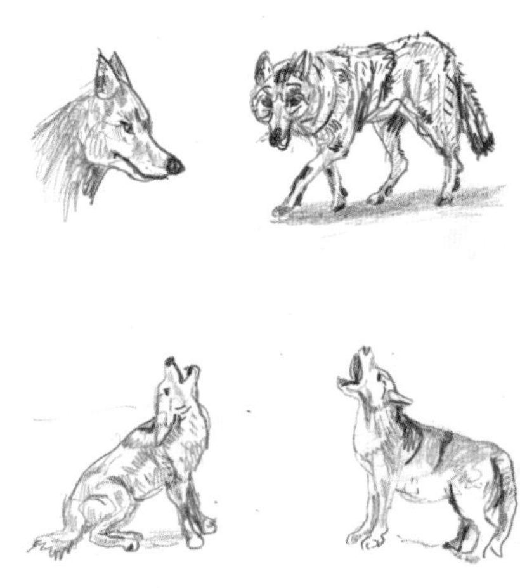

Before I taught in art schools, I remember trying to think what it would be like to talk with a student in front of their paintings. My image was of myself in corduroys, puffing slowly on a pipe, making lots of smoke, but not saying very much. The silences were supposed to convey something. I have never smoked a pipe or stood much in silence. So Joseph Beuys's famously enigmatic teaching style was probably better than mine.

14

AN UNFORTUNATE INCIDENT IN BARBARA HEPWORTH'S STUDIO

Modern art tends to be seen by cartoonists as a series of jokes. Those who make these jokes have often been trained in the same art schools as the successful fine artists who are their targets. Envy lies not far behind the caricature. The serious artist is fair game, because the nature of the business is about parading to the public a subjective statement. The actor can blame the playwright, the musician the composer, but the artist has nowhere to hide. It is naked exposure. We expect something outrageous from the privileged artist. The public loved Carl Andre's bricks – the piece confirmed all their prejudices.

So although I include a hole joke, I like the work of Hepworth. It gives me pleasure to walk round Battersea Park, stop at the south side and look at Hepworth's *Single Form* with the lake beyond. I have always thought of myself as a sculptor manqué, but the nearest I have come to that is to be living and working in the former studio of the sculptor Charles Sargeant Jagger (1885–1934).

St Ives comes in for a bit of stick in my picture. Despite becoming a Royal Academician, I have never been a joiner of groups and the idea of an artists' colony fills me with horror. I would rather join an ant colony than an artists' colony. I was a Sunday school and Cub Scout refusenik, as well as successfully avoiding team sports. The overzealous and overheated artistic atmosphere of St Ives does not appeal to me. I am sure there was a moment when Barbara Hepworth, passing Alfred Wallace, tipped

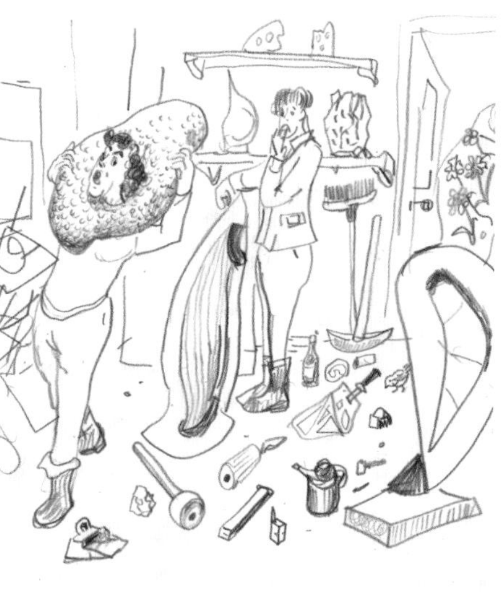

him a friendly nod and all in the garden was lovely. Recently a parking space in central St Ives was auctioned for a fortune. My Protestant gloom ethic suggests to me that artists in colonies have too much sunshine and too many delicious fish suppers.

A long while ago when I was touring Ireland I stayed in a Galway bed and breakfast (7s6d a night) and woke in the morning to find a large dead seagull in the washbasin. The seagull, for me, is an ominous bird.

15
POSADA ON FIRE

It was the Surrealists who rediscovered José Guadalupe Posada, the Mexican populist printmaker who chronicled everyday life at the time of the Mexican Revolution. He was a one-man band – artist, printer and distributor – who used engraved and cut woodblocks to produce, from a tiny workshop in Mexico City, broadsheets that dramatised life, and especially death. His prancing and amorous cadavers are both frightening and hopeful at the same time. But for the ubiquitous distribution of his graphic works he would have sunk without trace. He was buried in a pauper's grave. Only one photo of him, standing in front of his workshop, exists.

Easily reproducible, his designs spread like wildfire. I decided against using the skeletons in my version because they distract too much. In my drawing, three women are fighting it out in the street. Posada's women are always in action, murdering, loving and dancing. Posada's trousers are on fire from the studio stove. Why is he on fire? The old school-ground taunt 'Liar, liar, pants on fire' comes to mind. Do all Artists lie? Yes, in the service of truth. All pictures reflect and edit the reality around them. Storytelling has always served a serious purpose.

The Surrealists wanted to turn art history on its head and saw in Posada a hero. From Le Douanier Rousseau to Grandma Moses, artists who have had no formal training have been appreciated for their straightforward approach to the business. They cut to the chase.

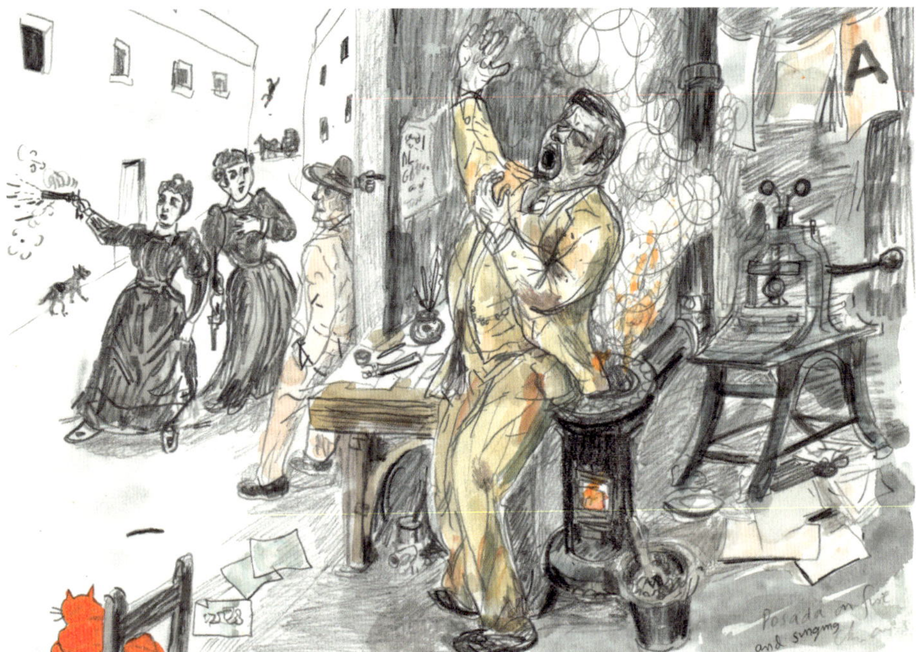

16
WALTER SICKERT FINDS A FLY IN HIS SOUP

He was not the Ripper, just a bit of a curmudgeon. Unlike many of my artists he has got something down on his canvas. He wants to clothe the nude and try his hand at Cubism. The Camden Town bedsitter looks like some of my rented rooms in North Kensington, before I became a proud homeowner. I have always enjoyed furnishing imaginary rooms to describe the inhabitants' moods. Sickert's room has that beige aura – the product of damp and tobacco – that lurks in so many rented rooms.

Becoming a painter in the Camden Town School was almost an option when I was first at art school. There was just enough post-war depression around to suggest that the tawdry bedsitter was a reasonable subject, and that a palette of murky colours was in some way appropriate. The nude model adorning the artist's studio was a persistent trope, but I never found anybody even half-way willing to participate.

I remember a fellow student once boasting to me that he could peel bits off the wallpaper while making love. In my picture Walter is only concerned with his mulligatawny. The miserable life of a painter, as forecast to me, involved working for years without recognition in horrible circumstances. However, there were privileged artists who at the end of the day put on their penguin suits and went to the Royal Academy for a slap-up dinner. If they lived in squalid digs it had some advantages: the cabbie might not expect a large tip and patrons felt they were on a rescue mission.

17

THE FAUVES' PICNIC

In an art history lesson, I was told that being a painter today was very difficult. The best time to have been in the second-oldest profession was to have been a Fauve at the start of the twentieth century. The 'wild beasts' were so called because of their bold use of colour and free attitude to representation. By implication, the style is supposed to be easier than others. I am not convinced. The principal artists involved were André Derain, Albert Marquet, Raoul Dufy and Henri Matisse, though like many supergroups they soon split up and went their own ways. Their subversion of naturalistic colour is sometimes quoted as being a response to the rise of effective colour reproduction in print and film. Also, the manufacture of powerful synthetic colour for use on buildings transformed the meagre palette of the nineteenth-century urban environment. Artists understood this seismic shift in colour technology.

I imagine the Fauves going on a picnic and adopting the pose of Manet's *Dejeuner sur l'herbe*. The picnic is an excuse to run riot with the colour pot. This is a *tableau vivant*, a snapshot. Artists like to pose for their photograph. There seems to be a security in belonging to a group – it is almost *de rigeur* to band together around a new idea. From Der Blaue Reiter to the YBAs, artists have espoused individuality while forming groups. Well, it is a lonely job, but if you were a Surrealist, would you want André Breton policing your output and excommunicating you?

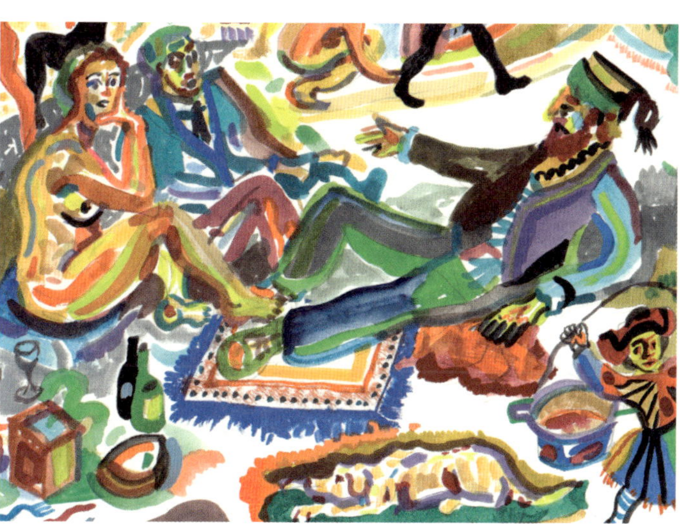

18

AN INDIAN MINIATURIST ENJOYS THE HEAT

As a boy I was enthralled by anything Indian. I was infatuated with Sabu the Elephant Boy from the Saturday Morning Pictures, and when it came to a fancy dress parade, I put together my own version of Indian costume, remarking to my mother that I understood why Indian people wore turbans and carried beaded sticks. I forget my reasoning. Much later I discovered, to my excitement, that I just might have some Indian blood in me from my great great grandfather. I made a print in 1997, 'My tiger is only sleeping', that depicts me returning in triumph on an elephant into a fantasy Delhi. I haven't been to India yet.

The Indian miniaturist in my painting is very small; he sits in yet another version of the studio, surrounded by the objects of his trade. After looking on Google at a lot of punkah wallahs and their contraptions I decided to invent my own version, which seems to owe something to a mangle, an etching press and a flying carpet.

Does the experience of being an artist share some common elements in different cultures? I have been liberal with my artists in giving them some of the same objects, from the cricket bat to the little cart. I suggest a fraternity in the studio. Van Gogh stated that the greatest fear a painter has is the blank canvas. Many of my artists, including my Indian miniaturist, have yet to make a start. Writer's block must be the same kind of thing.

As I have progressed with the series of paintings I have become more interested in painting itself. Up till now it has usually

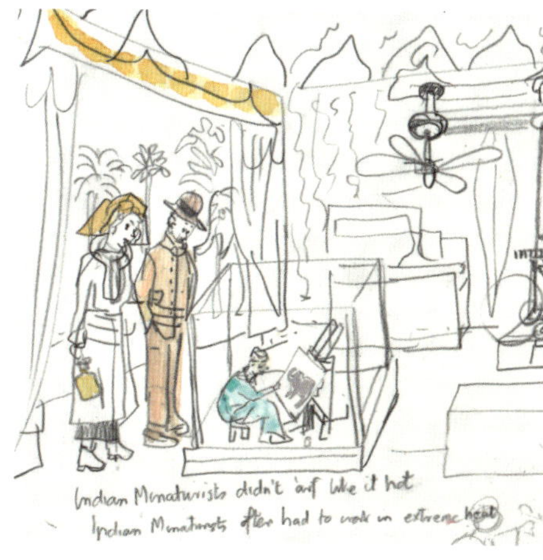

been a means to an end, but I have begun to find myself painting space and using colour for its own sake. The purpose of the paint is no longer to simply tell the story, it has become something to say in its own right. I have begun to relax about the narrative and the meaning. A lot of what you see is there to fulfil the pictorial logic. There is no real explanation for these pictures, they have come into being and will have to be judged on their own terms.

19

THE DIVINE COMEDY – REGINALD MARSH AT CONEY ISLAND

For me, it started in Dreamland Margate, when I was very small. I have a fascination with funfairs, despite being afraid of their raucous and bizarre nature. Riding a roller coaster is not my idea of fun. The head honcho of the British Roller Coaster Society bought one of my prints and told me that they hire coasters for a week and just ride round and round and round. My idea of hell.

In his paintings and etchings Reginald Marsh gave us a vision of a dystopian 'utopia' in Manhattan and on Coney Island Beach. The gothic idea comes to mind of the horror that delights whilst it saddens. There are photographs of Marsh drawing at Coney Island, dressed in a grey flannel suit – a very different outfit to the holidaymakers. He stands like Dante on his epic journey, observing the bodies of the tormented souls around him.

By the time I got to Coney Island in 2010 it was past its peak and subject to the attention of preservationists (I donated a print for fundraising). The funfair was a shadow of its former self. Marsh, like many other artists, saw himself as a reporter and commentator on his times. The devil has all the best tunes, and Marsh enjoys describing the dark side. Dante's epic poem is more interesting in its description of suffering than heaven.

Socially concerned artists abounded in New York in the 1930s, and when I was searching in my student days for meaning to cling onto in the storm of new waves of painting, I discovered the Ashcan School

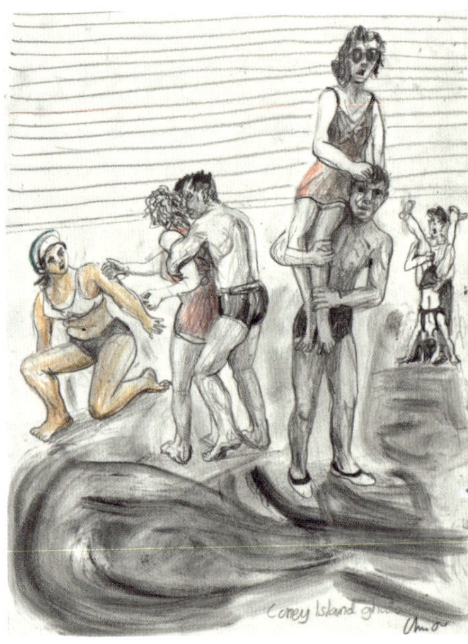

and the many artists who chronicled America's history. Reginald Marsh, with his passion for depicting theatres, railroads, factories and beaches, appealed to me. Here was a directness and respect for detail, whether it was locomotives or ladies' underwear, that I empathised with.

When I began the *Miserable Lives*, Marsh was a prime candidate. He is little known today. When I enquired in a New York bookshop for a monograph on him, people stared at me blankly. I finally got one as part of a stock disposal from the Olson Library at North Michigan University (50 cents plus postage and packing).

20

HOKUSAI'S TROUBLESOME UMBRELLA

Who invented the umbrella? Was it simply an adaptation of a sunshade that was an adaptation of a large leaf? My Hokusai has the world's worst umbrella. We have all seen those pathetic casualties in the street after a storm – abandoned frames with tattered rags clinging on like scraps of plastic in trees (some people call them witches' knickers). Hokusai is upright in a boat with a lady friend. His paints are at the ready, he is in the pose of an emergency aid worker or soldier ready to do his duty. He must stand and deliver.

A very formative experience for me was visiting China in 2004 and then Japan in 2006. The centre of the earth, according to the Chinese, is in Beijing. I had always thought it was somewhere in central London, or in a worst-case scenario, Paris. My mission in China was a commission, and I had to come up with some response. Luckily I was well trained and could draw what I saw. I quickly took to the streets of Beijing and Shanghai. My drawing became much more calligraphic and simple, in an attempt to deal with the multitude of sensations (most of which I didn't understand) from everywhere around me. I had my cultural revolution. After that, more visits to China and Japan continued to shift my centre of gravity. Strangely, wherever I draw, including China and Japan, people ask street directions of me assuming that I am part of the place. Drawing implies a kind of possession, which is why I was allowed to take photographs in Tiananmen Square in Beijing and Grand Central Station in New York, but drawing was strictly *verboten*.

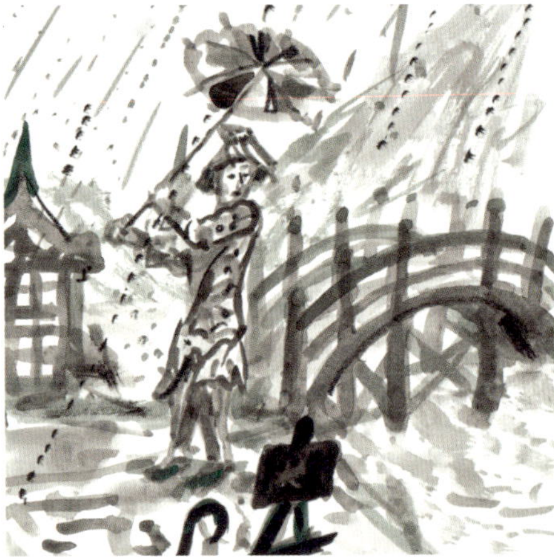

Hokusai's work has crossed every border. Although my work is quintessentially English, I aim to find audiences in different places. When an amateur theatre group puts on the *Mikado*, every trope of orientalism will be employed. Hokusai, in my picture, does not look particularly Japanese – more of a cross between Robinson Crusoe and Worzel Gummidge – but I did think the angled pen lines of rain showers set the scene, as well as the temple buildings on the horizon.

Hokusai drew every day; I try to do the same. It is not necessarily drawing to a pre-defined purpose, it is the exercise of the brain through pictorial description. It was John Ruskin's idea, in particular, that we should all draw. For some children it comes before speech – a way of configuring the relationship between things. To do it for all one's life is a great ambition and a privilege.

21

LOUISE BOURGEOIS WAS AWFULLY FOND OF TOAST

I did not want to feature spiders in Louise Bourgeois's studio. The shark may have been borrowed from Damien. I give her an obsession she most likely did not have – a fondness for toast and toasters. I see most of her exhibited work as leftovers from her studio. She saw printmaking as a way of remembering and forgetting, sculpture as a reconstruction of cages in which she had been imprisoned, writing a muffled cry for help. As with many of my artists, her studio is as much the work of art as the stuff it produces.

In the centre of turbulent cities studios are oases of calm and sanity (except perhaps for Francis Bacon's mess). The subtext of all the paintings in this book is about the studio life. Here is an extension of the brain – a human space where a rearrangement of the deckchairs is possible, and even sometimes the fabrication of something entirely new. Life in the studio is not necessarily dramatic. Making the tea and tidying up are important as well. The artist lives in the studio as well as working there. This is something of a conundrum for the art school. Can we train artists in these constrained times without giving them a studio that they can inhabit?

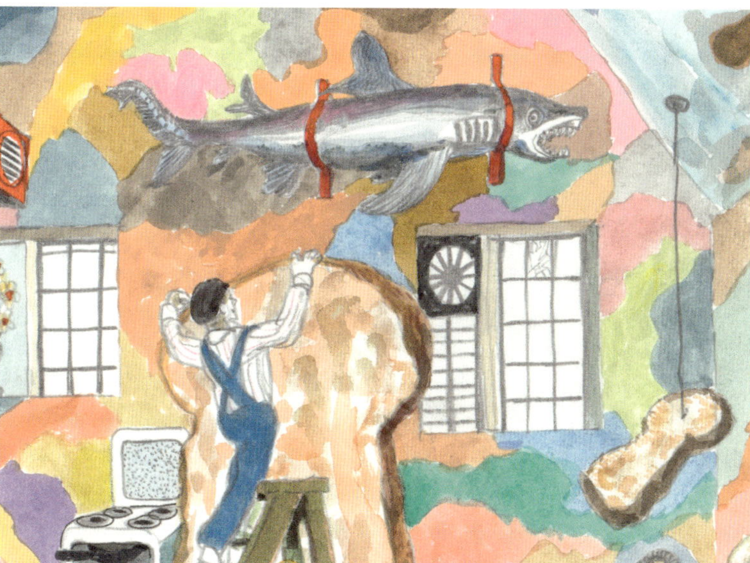

22

CANNY THOMAS BEWICK BY THE BANKS OF THE TYNE

I owe a great debt to Thomas Bewick. His engravings have provided me with explicit reference material over the years. Before the internet, there was an explosion of reproduced copyright-free material for artists, such as Dover Pictorial Archives, which gave us a wonderful list of source material from the Crystal Palace exhibition catalogue to Bewick's natural history. Engraved blocks have the beauty of clarity and objectivity, rendering information into a linear language, and they have remained the style for handbooks and medical instruction ever since.

Bewick's observations on his environment have a freshness and honesty, rather in the way the poet John Clare returns us to a purity of feeling. Catalogues have always fascinated me; they have no hierarchies and treat the mousetrap with equal care to the candelabra. The high-vis jacket stands alongside the wedding dress, and the fully paid-up fetishist can adore either or both.

On the use of references I have to admit nowadays to using Google to boost my range beyond books and memory, but there is such a thing as having too good a reference. Talking to illustration students at Kingston University once, I suggested that sub-standard references were better than extremely good ones. Imperfect information allows the artist to go freely to another kind of truth. I only just got out of that place alive. I still use an 85p jumble sale book – an A to Z of animals by Tibor Gergely – from which I can extemporise.

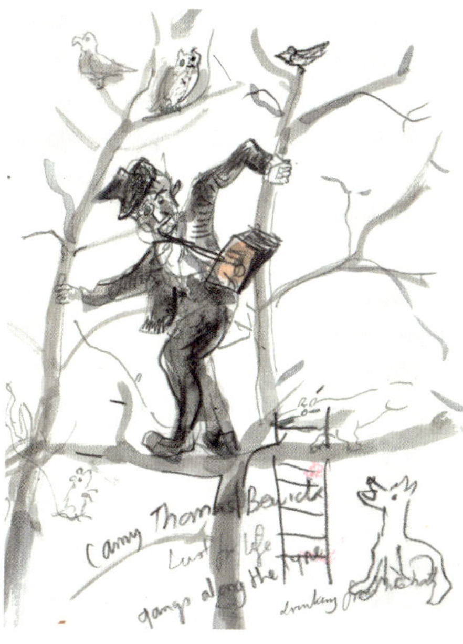

Here Thomas Bewick is on the banks of the Tyne, the English Huckleberry Finn, surrounded by many of the animals he was to immortalise. I have a collection of Sunderland pottery, which had its heyday shortly after the time of Bewick; it uses engraved and etched plates to make transfers that are put onto ceramics. Images such as the boat *Northumberland* (the vessel that took Napoleon to St Helena) feature, and this is visible behind Bewick in my drawing. In 2012 I did some experiments at the University of the West of England in an attempt to revive the technique. We got some good results but it went no further.

23

A CASE OF ZOOMANIA INVOLVING LEONORA CARRINGTON

Leonora Carrington wrote: 'Painting is like making strawberry jam very well.'

I am interested in zoos, but am not in favour of them. The zoo is a metaphor for many institutions (so it's perhaps not surprising that the Royal Academy should have a Keeper's House). Controlling wild beasts, from the menagerie to the wildlife park, seeks to turn the animals into passive attractions, not always with complete success. Leonora Carrington imagined people as untamed beasts. At an early age she was taken to Blackpool Zoo, and the transformation and transmutation of animals is one of her recurrent themes. In her short story *The Debutante* a hyena learns French very easily in order to substitute for the author as a debutante at a ball. Carrington was forced by her parents to go through the rituals of coming out in 1936, just before she ran away to Paris with Max Ernst.

As a student I read her short stories and shoved them to the back of my mind. I rediscovered them in 2017, and found that I had, unbeknown to myself, been using elements of them in my work for years. They had leached from my subconscious without attribution, particularly in my zoo pictures and my etching 'Once upon a warthog, a rich lady falls in love with a warthog'. Now I would like to give Carrington her rightful place in my canon of influences. Zoomania may or may not exist as a condition. A cure is not available on the National Health.

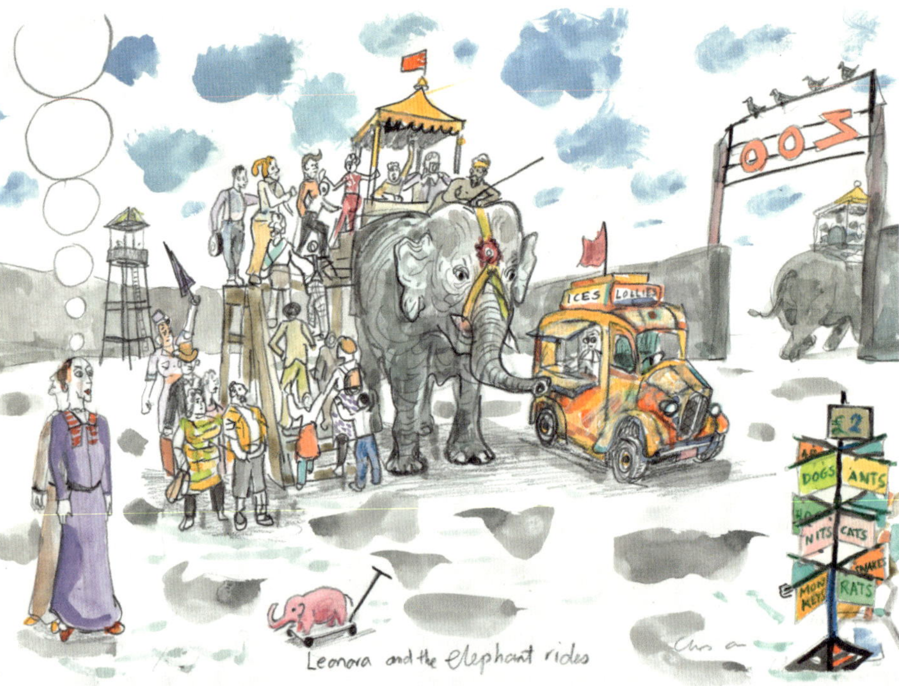

24

THINGS THAT GO BUMP IN THE NIGHT: REMBRANDT'S HAUNTED HOUSE

Rembrandt has that 'haunted' look in all his self-portraits. The ghost of himself is present haunting himself in his one hundred painted and etched self-portraits. The famous Bert Haanstra film made in 1956 dissolves chronologically the sequence from youth to old age. No artist has made so much of the self-portrait as Rembrandt, nor given us such a literal visual autobiography.

My Rembrandt lives in a dark, creaky house where things can easily go astray. In the shadows we are not quite sure what is going on. He welcomes a shaft of sunlight from one of the small windows. He is in a brown study. He is worrying about money, and something he put down and can't find. Rembrandt's fortunes rose and fell; he may or may not have been a good person with whom to be associated. In his novel about the artist, *Picture This*, Joseph Heller describes Rembrandt's ultimate test for any artist: painting a *trompe l'oeil* golden coin on the floor that visitors to the studio will be fooled into trying to pick up.

Rembrandt passes all the historical tests. Despite an introspective character and a reputation for meanness, he is one of the world's greatest artists. The paint is sublime but his printmaking may be one of the methods through which he gained this status. The unlimited editions of prints (still affordable today, if in a rather worn state) have reached every corner of the globe. They carry his humanity in every stroke of the etching needle. He treated his printmaking as an absolutely natural extension of his draughtsmanship.

25
DONALD MCGILL UP BEFORE THE BEAK AGAIN

High and low in art have often been fascinatingly intertwined. In the 1960s we fell in love with cheap advertising and popular culture. We dug down, not up. The history of art seemed largely to be the province of the upper classes. After reading George Orwell's essay 'The Art of Donald McGill' I became an enthusiast for the saucy postcards that were abundantly available at the seaside and have since become collector's items, especially the ones that were banned for obscenity. McGill was in court several times accused of corrupting morals by his work and courtroom scenes feature in jokes such as the one in speech bubbles in my painting. My courtroom merges into a musical hall, where McGill was also very much at home.

Growing up in suburban South London my family had a few gramophone records of classical music but we had no art on the walls. There was no art in our attic. The gallery lay beyond our pale. Poetry was in the past, or at best on the fringes. I thrived on comics, radio programmes and cinema. We spent time as a family looking at the annual *Giles* album from the *Daily Express*, which we regarded as a work of genius. I did graduate to Ronald Searle and especially liked his version of *The Rake's Progress* about the artist (the downfall is his election to the Royal Academy!). Television, when it came, was so small and blurred that it left little trace in my mind. Theatre was amateur theatricals, where the scenery fell over and you knew all the actors anyway. Music in general came from 'The Light Programme'.

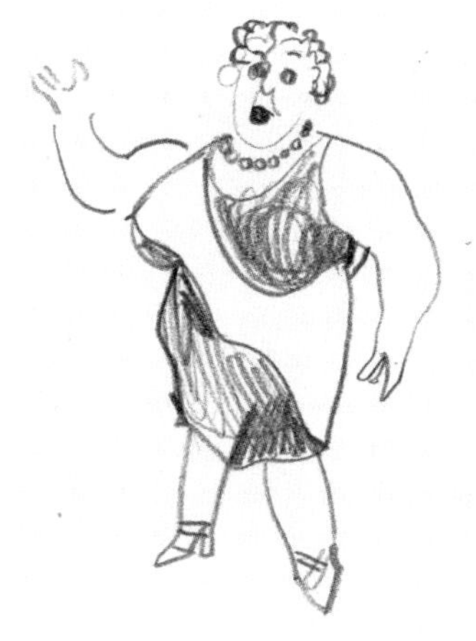

Art school was confusing; we were expected to appreciate Botticelli and Titian. Imagine my joy when I discovered counter culture and that Donald McGill was an unappreciated master (the so-called Picasso of the Pier) and that the Ealing Comedy films were swooned over by French intellectuals in *Cahiers du Cinéma*. I realised I need not desert the iconographic world of my youth after all.

Deep in me is the thread of English and European populism. Looking at the grotesque carvings of the Hereford School of Romanesque Sculpture from the twelfth and thirteenth centuries in places like Kilpeck, I can see connections to what I do. This groundswell of iconographic perversity stretches through the centuries and I claim to be part of it.

26
A SCULPTOR IN THE VALLEY OF THE KINGS MAKES A MISTAKE

I haven't been to Egypt, but I have seen *The Ten Commandments* and *Ben Hur* in CinemaScope. From the Grand Tour to Hollywood, Egypt has been a staple subject for the curious connoisseur. Failure dogs most artists, but the price of a mistake is usually personally absorbed. However, I imagine that under the pharaohs in the sixteenth to the eleventh century BC any error could be fatal. Chip off a nose and you could be in big trouble. When teaching in art schools I have emphasised the importance of 'failure' as a method of evolving solutions to the knotty problems that beset the creative artist. The edict that there is no progress in art leaves the artist dealing with the less obvious conundrums. Not the technical problems (how to sharpen a pencil etc); they need the correct solution. It is more the problem of what is good or bad in art. It is not a question with an easy answer. Just look at the trouble the Nazis got themselves into with that.

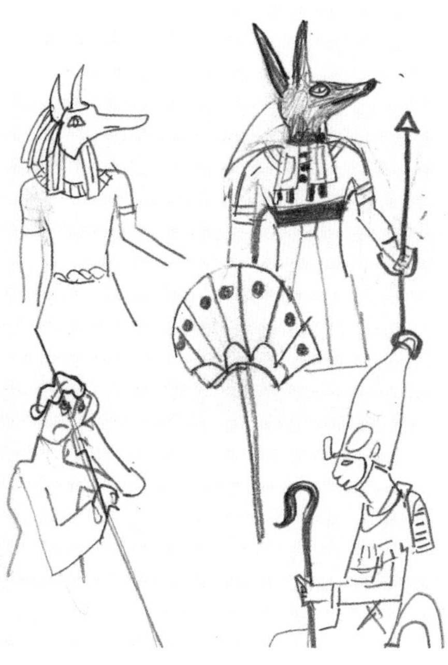

The accomplished traveller is supposed to have seen the seven wonders of the world, but that list is subjective. I have no lust for the Hanging Gardens of Babylon or the Colossus of Rhodes, neither of which exist anymore, but I would like to see the Valley of the Kings (which is not one of the original seven). The sculptors who laboured there must have had the most miserable lives. I nearly got a job when I left the Royal College of Art in 1967 drawing in Egypt for archaeologists recording discoveries. Was it the Six Day War that put the kibosh on that? Instead, I went to Cardiff College of Art to teach Foundation Studies.

27

THE DISCOMFORT OF CHARLES RENNIE MACKINTOSH

Tragically, Mackintosh's masterpiece, the Glasgow School of Art, was badly damaged in a fire in 2014. Hopefully it will be fully restored. My first experience of the place was, as a young graduate, being asked to come up from London to give a talk to 'a few' students. There was a buffet lunch washed down with generous measures of whisky. I must have met some Scottish bigwigs. Then I was ushered through a small door into what I remember as a vast lecture theatre packed with hundreds of people. This was the first time I had ever done a public talk about my work. Without the whisky I might never have gone over the top. I got through it, but nobody could say that it was my finest hour. Talking about my work, like writing about it, has always been important for me. I suffer under the impression that my best lecture was at the Beijing Central Academy in 2004 – there was a translator and the audience laughed at every one of my jokes. Of course, I have no idea how they were translated.

Then I found myself in 1982 becoming External Examiner in Printmaking at the Glasgow School of Art. At that time a member of staff was dismissed for refusing to obey the ban on smoking in the building. A very prescient action, though not enough. The 2014 blaze was caused by a foam canister being ignited by an overheating projector. It raises the question of the suitability of precious buildings for the rough and ready trade of art education. Mackintosh's building, by the time I knew it, was half a museum and half an art school. Probably the best

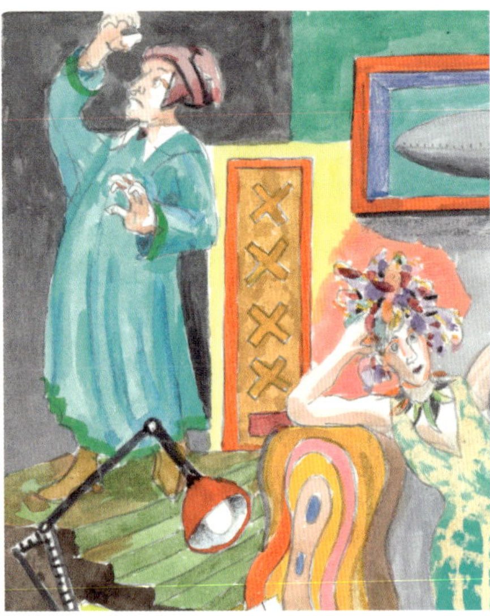

art school would be a bog-standard sturdy industrial building. When I went to Cuba I saw a very fancy art school building in Havana, sadly only half completed and abandoned because funds had run out. Architects beware! The art school and the artist's studio are for the dreams of the occupants not the builders.

Mackintosh made some rather beautiful paintings as well as being an architect and designer. So I understand his discomfort when I dump him in the Madonna Inn, in San Luis Obispo, California. I went there in 2013 for an hour or two on my trip down Highway 1. The colour, style and weird artefacts are reminiscent of Trump Tower. California challenges your taste buds in many ways.

28

BRIEF ENCOUNTER: L. S. LOWRY MEETS BERYL COOK

A chance meeting on a street corner between the Rent Collector and the Queen of Voluptuousness.

At nine years old I first went north and saw the industrial haze. Arriving at the Royal College of Art in the 1960s, I felt rather ashamed because I didn't have a northern accent or a working class pedigree. The success of gritty realism made us southerners feel a bit outclassed. It wasn't grim enough down south. The first fuzzy black-and-white episodes of Coronation Street left me with a pleasurable chill; I never watched it again after it went into colour. I did however, once meet Hilda Ogden (Jean Alexander). On my epic canal trip round inner Britain in 1978 I saw the last knockings of metal bashing in the Midlands and soot redistribution in the North. Also on my radar were northern comedians, schooled in the music hall tradition. My hero was and still is Ken Dodd – he can veer from the crass to the profound effortlessly. The verbal gymnastics of jokes have continued to be source of pleasure and an inspiration. I have entertained the notion that my work is equivalent to that of a stand-up comedian. The danger is it can be quickly dismissed as 'comic', but inside every comedian there is a serious person. I try to work both ends of the spectrum.

I have always had a strong sense of opposites. So who would I imagine L. S. Lowry meeting on a street corner? Certainly not Giacometti. My Picasso

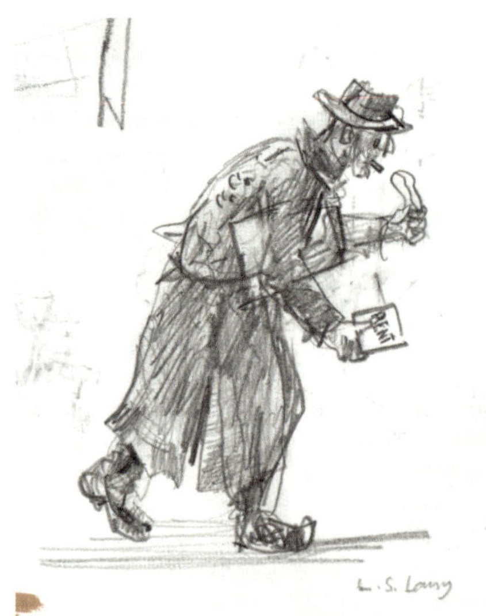

may fail to charm the women, but my Lowry gets a full-blown Beryl Cook. Not the flesh-and-blood Beryl, who in photographs looks nothing like her creations, but one of her larger than life imagined characters.

29

HIERONYMUS BOSCH – TIME TRAVELLER

In 2014 I went to Holland to see the most complete exhibition of Bosch paintings ever assembled. Getting tickets was difficult and the exhibition very crowded. You could hardly see the paintings. I was struck by the demeanour of the predominately middle class, older audience. Bosch, as far as we can tell, wanted his paintings to be instructive of the realities of Hell. *The Garden of Earthly Delights* (Museo del Prado, Madrid) is not an enjoyable romp through crazy things, but an excoriating labyrinth of grotesques meant to scare you into righteousness. My audience, however, look as though they are having rather a good time, snapping away on their iPhones to send images to their friends. Perhaps, as with many cultural events, it was part of a tick list of achievements. In other words, Bosch failed in his primary intention. He arrives as a time traveller, stripped of his message. Or perhaps, unconsciously, he knew another world would come to pass.

Unlike my other Fabulous Artists, Bosch does not appear in the painting. He is too deeply buried in his work. The misery is the outcome. The audience wander, happily bewildered through an environment of shapes and colours. I was very struck on my visit by the presence of a partially sighted man being guided around. It was easy to discover resemblances to Bosch's strange characters in some of the spectators. Did Bosch unwittingly or intentionally have drug-fuelled visions? Maybe it is only too easy to step into the phantasmagoric, in either the Middle Ages or today?

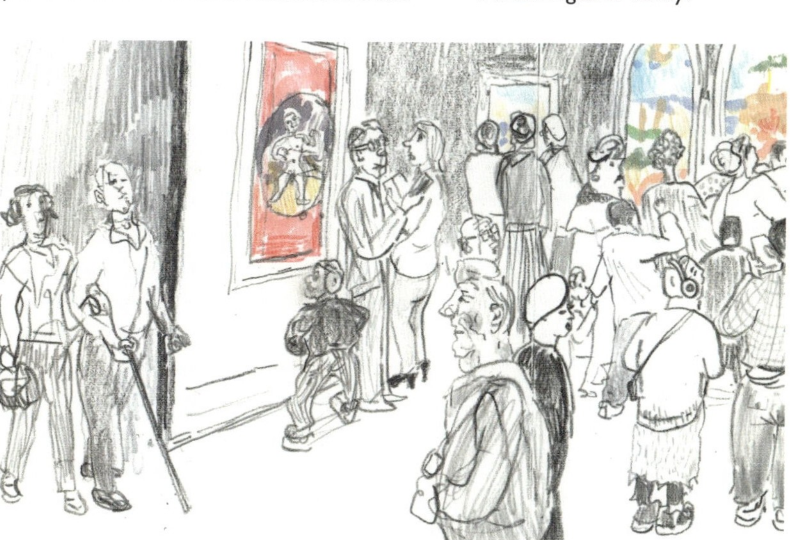

30

GOYA IN BORDEAUX

At the end of his life Goya went into exile in Bordeaux. Artists don't retire, and the final years of his life were very productive. The bullfighting lithographs and his albums of drawings shown at the Courtauld Gallery in 2015 reveal a wonderfully creative old age.

My Goya has a little cart to transport his paintings that he is stumbling along with, much as he always has done throughout his life. At the centre of the painting is a lithographic press with a stone on it. The press is a later model than the one that Goya used. It is my nineteenth-century French wooden press (ex Editions Alecto), now in retirement. I am addicted to lithography for much the same reasons as Goya, I love its powerful graphic verisimilitude.

Lithography was invented in 1796 by Alois Senefelder, an out-of-work Austrian actor and music copyist. The process depends on the chemical antipathy of grease and water. It is sometime known as 'chemical printing', because it depends on chemistry to define the printing matrix rather than raised or recessed areas of the block. The image can be drawn straight onto the stone by the artist, and the brush and drawing marks can be directly printed onto paper, giving veracity and control to the artist's intentions. An exact ghost of the artist's work can be achieved. The original method using limestone blocks (the best ones quarried in Bavaria) is still practised by artists who appreciate the multitude of effects that can be achieved. Masters of lithography have included Käthe Kollwitz, Picasso, Munch, Jim Dine and David Hockney. Lithography, through developments like photography and mechanisation of presses, went on to be one of the world's most ubiquitous printing mediums for commercial reproduction.

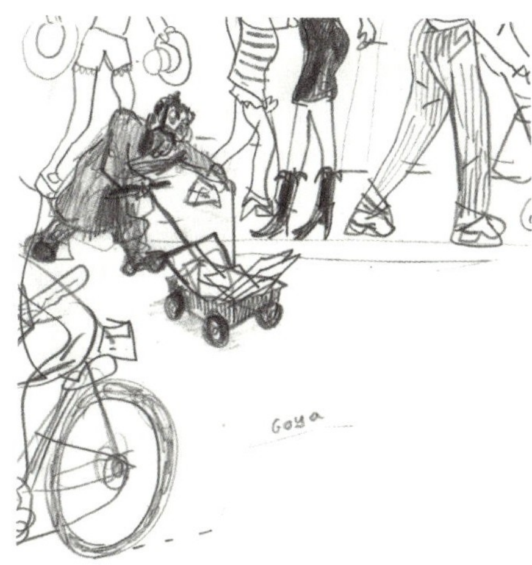

My Goya in Bordeaux puts the maestro into a mad world. The Citroen 2CV, the side of beef and *Les Demoiselles D'Avignon* have no direct connection to him, but as with all my Fabulous Artists there will only be six degrees of separation to the subsequent cultural developments. Artists are, by virtue of their pursuits, partly detached from the worlds they inhabit, reaching into both the past and the future.

Royal Academy Publications
Florence Dassonville
Alison Hissey
Rosie Hore
Carola Krueger
Peter Sawbridge
Nick Tite

Design: Jon Kielty
Typeset in Gill Sans

Photography: DawkinsColour (John Bodkin), London
Printed in Wales by Gomer Press

British Library Cataloguing-in-Publication Data
A catalogue record for this book is available from the British Library

ISBN 978-1-910350-89-8

Distributed outside the United States and Canada by
ACC Publishing Group, Sandy Lane, Old Martlesham,
Woodbridge, Suffolk 1P12 4SD

Distributed in the United States and Canada by
ARTBOOK | D.A.P., 155 Sixth Avenue, New York
NY 10013

The paintings from 'The Miserable Lives of Fabulous Artists' series were shown in the Belle Shenkman Room of the Keeper's House at the Royal Academy of Arts in 2018.

'Zoomania' is a colour lithograph published jointly by the Artist and the Royal Academy and is available from www.royalacademy.org.uk/artsales or call 0800 634 6341.

'Searching for a lost button at Jackson's', a lithograph and silkscreen published by the artist, can be viewed with more of Chris Orr's prints, paintings and drawings at www.chrisorr-ra.com.